HOUSE of WHITE BIRCHES

QUICK & EASY
Christmas CRAFTS™

Edited by Laura Scott

HOUSE of
WHITE
BIRCHES
PUBLISHERS
SINCE 1947

Quick & Easy Christmas Crafts

Editor: Laura Scott
Pattern Editor: Lāna Schurb
Associate Editor: June Sprunger
Copy Editor: Cathy Reef
Technical Artist: Allison Rothe
Publication Coordinator: Myra Moore
Design Coordinator: Tanya Turner

Photography: Tammy Christian, Jennifer Fourman, Jeff Chilcote
Photography Stylist: Arlou Wittwer
Photography Assistant: Linda Quinlan

Production Coordinator: Brenda Gallmeyer
Book Design/Production: Dan Kraner
Production Assistants: Shirley Blalock, Dana Brotherton, Carol Dailey
Traffic Coordinator: Sandra Beres

Publishers: Carl H. Muselman, Arthur K. Muselman
Chief Executive Officer: John Robinson
Marketing Director: Scott Moss
Editorial Director: Vivian Rothe
Production Director: George Hague

Printed in the United States of America
First Printing: 1999
Library of Congress Number: 99-94088
ISBN: 1-882138-44-9

Every effort has been made to ensure the accuracy and completeness of the instructions in this book. However, we cannot be responsible for human error or for the results when using materials other than those specified in the instructions, or for variations in individual work.

A note from the Editor

Dear Crafters,

When I was given the challenge of serving as editor of this book, I spent several days with my Christmas thinking cap on. Before long, the entire Craft It Christmas theme took shape in my mind. Trim It Christmas. Wear It Christmas. Wrap It Christmas. Not only did these phrases sound catchy, but they also seemed like great chapter titles!

From that point on, the book quickly took shape as our freelance designers began to work. My staff and I were very impressed with the designers' display of talent, whimsy, warmth and skill that came shining through in their original designs. Forty designers contributed to this volume. Their projects cover a range of craft techniques and styles. Another noteworthy fact about this collection is that, true to the book's title, the projects included can be made quickly and easily. If by the third week of December you find yourself short on time and money, yet still long on your Christmas shopping list, then this book will prove to be a lifesaver, not to mention a time-saver and money-saver. Although we have a specific chapter for holiday gifts, any of the projects would actually make great gifts. (Who wouldn't appreciate a charming set of handcrafted ornaments as a gift, for example?)

From the designers who created such fresh and original Christmas projects and the skilled editors who wrote easy-to-follow instructions, to the photographers who set up each picture with style and finesse and the graphic artists who pulled all the elements together into 176 attractive pages, we've all enjoyed bringing together this festive collection. We hope you enjoy crafting and sharing each of these merry projects with friends and family for many years to come.

Warm regards,

Laura Scott

Contents

nts

Trim It Christmas

Tree Trims & Ornaments

Few events bring as much excitement to a family as picking out a Christmas tree, bringing out the ornaments and garlands, and getting ready to decorate the best tree ever! Whet the family's appetite for this anticipated event all year round as you craft delightful ornaments each and every family member will love!

Cheery Snowmen Ornaments

Designs by Chris Malone

Materials

Snowman With Earmuffs

- 2 (¾") green pompoms
- 4" black wire
- 4" square red felt
- Red sewing thread

Snowman With Cap

- 3" x 6" piece black velour
- ⅜" black pompom
- 2" green wreath
- 1" piece artificial green bough
- Red berry floral pick

Each Snowman

- 6" x 9" piece white knit fleece or velour
- Fabric-marking pencil
- 1" x 9" strip plaid flannel
- 8 (3mm) black beads
- Pointed bamboo skewer
- Powdered cosmetic blusher
- Cotton swab
- Orange acrylic paint
- Paintbrush
- Sparkle Glaze by Delta Technical Coatings
- Polyester fiberfill
- 2 (2½") twigs
- Sewing machine
- Sewing thread: white and black
- Tacky craft glue
- Low-temperature glue gun

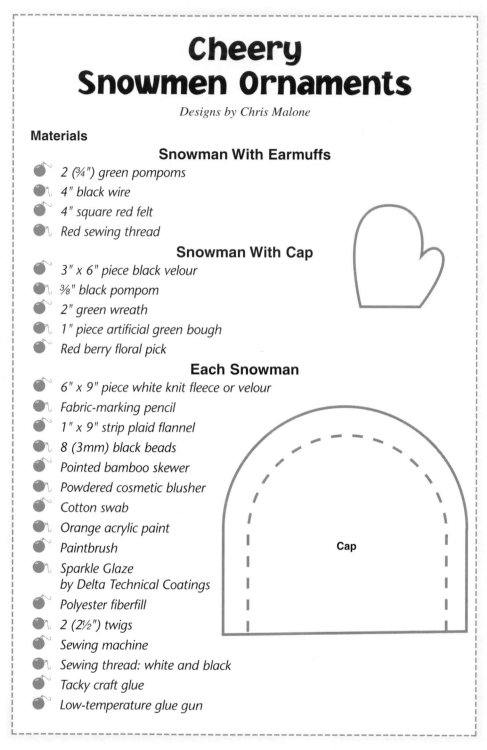

Cap

Project Note

Refer to photo for placement.

Instructions

1. Fold white fleece in half, right sides facing. Referring to pattern (page 9), trace one body onto doubled fleece. Pin doubled fleece together to keep it from shifting.

2. Thread sewing machine with white thread; sew all around traced snowman, stitching on traced line.

Cut out snowman, cutting ⅛" from stitched line. Clip curves. Carefully cut a slash at neckline through one side of snowman, taking care not to cut through stitching. Turn right side out through this opening.

3. Stuff snowman with fiberfill, inserting it through opening at neck. Slipstitch opening closed.

4. Using black thread, sew on two beads for eyes, knotting ends of thread at neck where they will be hidden by scarf. Apply powdered blusher to cheeks with cotton swab. Sew six beads to face for smile; when all beads are secured, run black thread back through all beads in a continuous line.

5. Paint pointed end of skewer with orange paint; let dry. Cut ¾"-long tip off pointed end. Using small, sharp, pointed scissors, make a tiny hole in middle of face; apply dot of glue to blunt end of skewer point and insert into hole.

6. Fringe ¾" of one end of plaid flannel strip. Wrap scarf around snowman's neck, tying at one side.

7. Using small, sharp, pointed scissors, make a tiny hole through front layer of snowman at side. Apply glue to bottom ½" of twig; insert into hole for arm. Repeat on other side.

8. Thin Sparkle Glaze with water as needed so it will spread thinly. Using paintbrush, apply glaze to *parts* of snowman, scarf, arms and accessories—do not cover completely. Let dry. If desired, apply a second

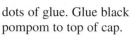

dots of glue. Glue black pompom to top of cap.

3. Glue wreath to one twig arm. Cut berries from floral pick, leaving ⅛"–¼" stems. Glue berries around the wreath.

4. Glue end of bough into roll of cap; glue three berries at base of bough.

These whimsical ornaments are sure to bring a smile to your face as you make them, and to your family's faces as they share them!

coat to some areas; let dry.

Earmuffs & Mittens

1. Bend wire in curve; hot-glue tips of wire to sides of head. Glue green pompoms to head over wire tips.

2. Fold red felt in half, wrong sides facing; trace two mittens (page 8) onto doubled felt. Pin doubled felt together to keep it from shifting.

3. Thread sewing machine with red thread; sew around mittens, stitching on traced lines and leaving bottoms open. Cut out mittens, cutting ⅛" from stitching. Glue mittens over ends of twig arms.

Cap & Wreath

1. Cut two caps (page 8) from black velour. Pin pieces together, right sides facing. Thread sewing machine with black thread and sew hats together along curved edge using ¼" seam allowance; leave bottom (straight edge) open. Trim seam allowance to ⅛"; clip curves and turn hat right side out. Turn bottom edge under ¾"; finger-press. Turn folded bottom edge *to outside* ¼" to make finished roll at bottom of cap. Tack roll in place with needle and thread.

2. Place cap on snowman's head at an angle; secure with

Slash

These delightful angels are the treasure at the end of a rainbow! Craft them in cheerful, bright colors to liven up your Christmas tree!

Project Notes

A purchased precut wooden shape sometimes sold as a mustache may be substituted for the plywood wings.

Refer to photo throughout for placement.

Rainbow Angels

Designs by Chris Malone

Materials
Each Ornament

- 1¼" wooden half-bead
- 5" x 2" piece ¼"-thick plywood (see Project Note)
- Band saw or scroll saw
- Sandpaper
- Acrylic paints: skin tone, black, red and bright color for wings
- Paintbrush
- Satin-finish varnish
- 2" x 6" piece white felt
- 2" x 4" piece yellow felt
- Felt scraps: green and 3 other assorted bright colors
- 6-strand embroidery floss: light green, white, gold and bright color to match wings
- Embroidery needle
- 8" ⅛"-wide white ribbon
- 8" ⅛"-wide ribbon in bright color to match wings
- Small amount of white mini-curl doll hair
- Polyester fiberfill
- Powdered cosmetic blusher
- Cotton swab
- Toothpick
- Glue stick
- Low-temperature glue gun

Wings & Head

1. Referring to patterns throughout, cut one wing piece from ¼" plywood; sand wings and wooden half-bead thoroughly.

2. Paint wings on all surfaces with bright color of paint; let dry. Apply second coat; let dry.

3. Paint wooden half-bead with skin tone paint; let dry. Using toothpick, apply tiny dots of black paint for eyes and red paint for mouth. Let dry. Apply cosmetic blusher to cheeks with cotton-tip swab.

4. Apply satin-finish varnish to all surfaces of head and wings; let dry.

Body & Halo

1. Cut two bodies from white felt and two halos from yellow felt. Cut one set of four leaves from green felt, and one set of one small and two large circles for flowers from assorted bright colors. Arrange flowers and leaves on one body piece; tack in place with glue stick.

2. Using 2 strands white embroidery floss, attach flowers by sewing five straight stitches from center out; finish with French knot at center of each flower.

3. Using 2 strands light green embroidery floss, attach leaves to body with fly stitch (see diagram): Begin with single short straight stitch ¼" down leaf tip. Add three progressively larger fly stitches down to base of leaf and finish with short straight stitch to end of leaf.

4. Pin decorated body front to plain body back. Using 2 strands embroidery floss to match color of wings, blanket-stitch body halves together, stuffing lightly with fiberfill before closing.

5. Pin halo pieces together; join with blanket stitch worked around edge with 2 strands gold embroidery floss.

Finishing

1. Make hanging loop by folding white ribbon in half and hot-gluing ends to center front of wings.

2. Hot-glue bottom of halo to top back of head. Rub hair between fingers to "frizz." Hot-glue hair to head.

3. Tie colored ribbon in small bow, trimming ends at angle. Hot-glue bow to side of head.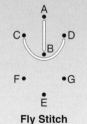

Fly Stitch
Begin at top (tip) row of stitches. Bring thread up at A, down at B, and up at C. Leaving a bit of slack, take thread down at D, then up at B behind C-D stitch; tighten gently to pull C-D stitch into Y shape without puckering. Take thread down at E, up at F, down at G, back up at E, etc.

Instructions

1. Referring to patterns throughout, cut two gingerbread pieces from tan felt for each boy and girl; draw mouths on two with marker. Referring to photo throughout, sew on 6mm beads for eyes using black thread. Using 3 strands white embroidery floss, backstitch mouths following lines drawn earlier.

2. Pin embellished gingerbread boy front to plain back; repeat with gingerbread girl pieces. Using 3 strands white embroidery floss, backstitch halves together around edges. Punch four circles from red craft foam using hole punch; glue circles to ends of smiles.

3. Following manufacturer's instructions, fuse webbing to wrong side of plaid fabric. For each ornament, trace one dress or one vest onto wrong side; cut out. Glue lace to bottom edge of dress; let dry. Trim lace evenly.

4. Glue dress to gingerbread girl and vest to gingerbread boy. Glue two buttons to front of dress and one button to vest.

5. Cut red grosgrain ribbon in half; tie each in a bow; trim ends at angles. Glue bows at neckline of dress and vest.

6. Cut green ribbon in half; fold each half into a loop; glue ends to center back of ornaments.

Attach lace here

Children will love helping you make these darling gingerbread boy and girl ornaments! Why not make a set for your child's schoolteacher?

Gingerbread Kids

Designs by Helen Rafson

Materials

- Tan felt
- Black sewing thread
- 4 (6mm) round black beads
- White 6-strand embroidery floss
- Scrap of red craft foam
- Fusible webbing
- Scraps of plaid fabric
- Tacky craft glue
- 3 (½") red buttons
- ¼" round hole punch
- 14" ¼"-wide red grosgrain ribbon
- 14" ⅛"-wide green satin ribbon
- 3" piece white lace

Instructions

1. Adhere double-sided adhesive to smooth side of corrugated cardboard pieces and to wrong sides of all other papers.

2. Referring to patterns, cut mitten and stocking from plaid paper and cuffs from polka-dot paper. Using pinking shears, trim edges of green paper.

3. Peel backing from adhesive on corrugated cardboard; press cardboard pieces together in pairs, smooth side to smooth side. Peel backing from green paper; press one piece to each corrugated pair.

4. Peel backing from stocking and cuff; press onto green paper. Repeat with mitten and cuff.

5. Using black marking pen, draw "running stitches" around edge of mitten and stocking.

6. Cut jute into two 11" pieces and two 9" pieces. Separate one 11" piece into individual strands; holding strands together, tie in a bow. Repeat with remaining 11" piece. Glue bow to front of each ornament.

7. Thread gold embroidery floss through holes in each button; knot floss on front of button, leaving ¼" ends; glue button over middle of each jute bow.

8. Knot ends of each 9" piece of jute to make hanging loop; glue loop to wrong side of each ornament. ❦

P aper crafting is fun when you have colorful paper in different textures to use! Craft these ornaments with plaid, polka-dot and cardboard paper!

Plaid Paper Ornaments

Designs by Deborah Spofford

Materials

- 4 (3" x 5") pieces corrugated cardboard
- 2 (2¾" x 4½") pieces green paper from Paper Pizazz
- 2 (3" x 5") pieces red plaid paper from Paper Pizazz
- 3" square red paper with white polka dots from Paper Pizazz
- 2 (½") green buttons
- 40" natural jute twine
- 2 (5" x 8") sheets double-sided adhesive
- Gold 6-strand embroidery floss
- Pinking shears
- Tacky craft glue
- Black fine-line permanent marking pen

delightfully
festive trio
of wood-
burned ornaments!

Project Notes

Read and follow all manufacter's instructions and safety warnings included with woodburner.

Refer to photo and patterns throughout for color placement.

Instructions

1. Referring to patterns (page 15), transfer markings to both sides of wooden ornaments.

2. Tape woodburner wire holder to work surface with masking tape. Use needle-nose pliers to insert flow point into woodburner and tighten it. Place burner in holder; plug in. Allow to heat for 5 minutes.

3. Holding woodburner as you would a pencil, burn over all pattern lines.

4. Use white and colored markers to color areas as desired, leaving some areas uncolored so wood shows. Let dry for 30 minutes.

5. Spray both sides of ornaments with two or more coats of clear matte-finish sealer; let dry.

6. Apply 3-D enhancer to selected areas and dry flat. (On sample projects, it is applied to ornaments on tree, to all natural-color areas, to leaves, to decorative bands and to clappers on bells.)

7. Hold together a length of green ribbon and a length of red; thread through hole in ornament and knot to make hanging loop; repeat for remaining ornaments. ✆

Country Wooden Ornaments

Designs by Betty Auth

Materials

- Walnut Hollow Large Laser-Cut Ornaments: double bell #12970, sleigh #12973 and tree #12972
- Walnut Hollow Creative Woodburner #5567 with Flow Point #5592
- Marvy LePlume II markers by Uchida: medium red #2, bright yellow #5, red orange #7, medium green #11, dark red #65, pale green #70 and dark green #72
- Arctic white Zig Woodcraft marker
- Aerosol clear matte-finish sealer
- Clear Royal Coat Dimensional Magic #2201 3-D enhancer from Plaid Enterprises, Inc.
- 3 (12") pieces ⅛"-wide red ribbon
- 3 (12") pieces ⅛"-wide green ribbon
- Masking tape
- Needle-nose pliers

*T*hese darling Santa Claus ornaments are sure to warm—and win—your holiday heart!

Project Note

Refer to photo throughout for placement.

Instructions

1. Make beard by wrapping yarn around two fingers of one hand. Slide loops off fingers and tie in center with 4" piece of yarn to form a loopy bundle. Repeat to make a total of seven loopy bundles for each face. Make another bundle in the same manner but cut loops at both ends to form mustache; repeat for second mustache.

2. Cut four ⅛" pieces yarn; using tacky white craft glue, glue two above each eye for eyebrows. Using hot-glue gun throughout, glue one ruby faceted bead to center of each face for nose. Glue seven bundles of yarn around bottom of each face; clip loops and trim to form beards. Glue mustache bundles under noses.

3. Referring to patterns throughout, cut two complete stocking shapes including cuff area and two mitten shapes from plain white felt. Cut two hats from red felt and two from kelly green felt; from kelly green, also cut one ¾"- wide strip. From white plush felt cut one mitten cuff and one stocking cuff; cut also two ¼" x 3" strips for hat cuffs.

4. Cut ¾"-wide green felt strip into rectangles; glue to front of one stocking in checkerboard pattern; when glue is dry, trim rectangles to follow stocking shape.

5. Glue green ribbon to front of one mitten to form striped pattern.

6. Glue together matching stocking and mitten pieces, applying glue to edges and leaving tops open to form pockets. Glue a cuff to top of front of each ornament.

7. Glue 11mm heart bead to each white square on stocking front. Glue 15mm heart to center of mitten; glue 4mm round ruby cabochons around 15mm heart.

8. Tie small bow in center of red ribbon; tie center of bow in knot to secure. Leave ends long; tie in knot 1" from end to form hanging loop. Repeat with remaining green ribbon.

9. Glue green bow to upper corner of mitten ornament; glue red bow to upper corner of stocking ornament.

10. Glue red hat pieces together along long edges, leaving end open; glue plush felt around bottom of hat for cuff; repeat with green hat pieces and remaining plush felt cuff. Glue or sew heart bead to end of green hat; glue or sew jingle bell to end of red hat.

11. Place hat on each head; pull tips of hats off to one side of face and glue to secure. Glue red-hat Santa to top of mitten; glue green-hat Santa to top of stocking.

Santa Pocket Ornaments

Designs by Vicki Blizzard

Materials

- 9" x 12" sheets Rainbow Classic Felt from Kunin Felt: red, kelly green and white
- 9" x 12" sheet white #550 Rainbow Plush Felt from Kunin Felt
- 2 large Create Your Own Expression Faces for Places #PT 30005 face buttons from True Colors International
- White Bumples textured yarn by One & Only Creations
- 2 (4mm) ruby faceted beads
- 10 (11mm) ruby smooth heart beads from The Beadery
- 15mm ruby smooth heart bead from The Beadery
- 8 (4mm) ruby round cabochons
- ⅜" gold jingle bell
- 1½ yards ⅛"-wide green satin ribbon
- 12" ⅛"-wide red satin ribbon
- Sewing thread and needle (optional)
- Tacky white craft glue
- Hot-glue gun

Corrugated cardboard, twine, wire and spare buttons can be crafted into a collection of charming ornaments in no time at all!

1. Referring to patterns (pages 19 and 20), trace one gingerbread man, one heart, one tree, one bell, one candy cane and two mittens onto smooth side of corrugated cardboard. Cut out. Embellish as follows, or as desired.

2. *Candy Cane:* Tie jute around candy cane in bow, securing with a dot or two of glue; glue a ½" red button over center of bow. Using needle, punch hole for hanger in top of ornament; thread with hanging loop of 22-gauge wire.

3. *Gingerbread Man:* Tie jute around neck in bow;

Quick-as-a-Wink Ornaments

Designs by Paula Bales

Materials

- Corrugated cardboard
- Assorted buttons: ½" red, ¾" green and 1" black
- 22-gauge wire
- Natural jute twine
- Christmasy plaid or print fabric scraps
- Needle
- 1½" wooden star shape
- Straw-gold acrylic paint
- Paintbrush
- Craft glue or hot-glue gun
- Craft drill with ¹⁄₁₆" bit

glue two ¾" green buttons down center. Using needle, punch hole for hanger in top of ornament; thread with 22-gauge wire. Form into hanging loop, leaving 2" ends; wrap wire ends around paintbrush handle to form decorative coils.

4. *Mittens:* Tie jute twine around wrists; glue three ½" red buttons across mitten cuffs. Using needle, punch hole for hanger in center of cuff edge on each mitten and hang on a "string" of 22-gauge wire, kinking wire as desired and coiling wire ends as for gingerbread man.

5. *Heart:* Thread ends of a 4" piece of wire through holes in black 1" button so both wire ends protrude to front; twist ends and coil around paintbrush handle. Glue button to center of heart cutout; glue hanging loop of jute twine to back.

6. *Bell:* Using needle, punch hole for hanging loop at top of ornament; thread with wire hanging loop. Tear a 12" x 1" strip of Christmas fabric; tie in double bow, trimming ends as desired. Glue to center top of bell.

7. *Christmas Tree:* Drill two holes in center of wooden star, as for a button. Paint star on all surfaces with straw-gold paint; let dry. Thread 6" length of wire through holes so both ends protrude from front; twist wire ends to secure, then coil ends around paintbrush handle. Glue star to center top of tree, catching ends of a jute twine hanging loop between star and cardboard. Glue three ¾" green buttons evenly spaced down front of tree. ✎

Nature's Beauty Ornaments

Designs by Creative Chi

Materials

Candy Cane

- 4¼" twig candy cane
- Botanicals from Creative Chi:
  3 red milo berry sprigs
  3 preserved boxwood sprigs
  Engelmann cone
  2 Casurina pods
  2 sprigs Canella berries
- 5 dried cranberries

Wreath

- 2¾" twig wreath
- Botanicals from Creative Chi:
  3 red milo berry sprigs
  5 preserved boxwood sprigs
  3 hemlock cones
  3 birch cones
  2 pieces dried ginger
- Filbert (hazelnut)
- 3 dried cranberries

Heart

- 2¾" x 3¼" twig
  heart-shaped wreath
- Botanicals from Creative Chi:
  2 red milo berry sprigs
  5 preserved boxwood sprigs
  3 hemlock cones
  2 sprigs Canella berries
  Star anise
- 3 dried cranberries

All Projects

- Low-temperature glue gun
- Brown #3 pearl cotton

Dried pinecones, berries, seeds and leaves arranged and glued onto shaped twig ornaments bring nature's beauty indoors.

Project Note

Refer to photo throughout for placement.

Instructions

1. Begin each ornament with preserved boxwood backgrounds; then add Canella berries or dried ginger.

2. Position center piece—Engelmann cone on candy cane, star anise on heart or filbert on wreath.

3. Fill in with remaining botanicals as shown in photo.

4. Tie hanging loop of #3 pearl cotton to each ornament.

Capture the elegance of cross stitch with this set of three ornaments. Accented with beads and stitched on beautiful fabric, they're sure to become family keepsakes used year after year!

Geometric Cross-Stitch Ornaments

Designs by Joan Beiriger

Materials
Each Ornament

- *DMC 6-strand embroidery floss as listed in color key*
- *Silver #001-BF blending filament from Kreinik*
- *#24 tapestry needle*
- *8" square 25-count metallic silver-and-white Lugana fabric by Zweigart*
- *Mill Hill glass beads from Gay Bowles Sales Inc. as listed in color key*
- *3" square cardboard from back of tablet, etc.*
- *3" square red felt*
- *White felt squares: 3", 2¾" and 2½"*
- *Fabric glue*

Stitching

1. Whipstitch or zigzag fabric edges to prevent unraveling. Find center of 25-count fabric by folding fabric in quarters and finger-pressing; mark center with pin or basting stitch if needed.

2. Matching center of fabric to center of graph, stitch design using 2 strands floss for Cross Stitches and 1 strand floss for Backstitch, and making each stitch over 2 fabric threads

3. When stitching is complete, attach beads as indicated using 2 strands of matching floss.

Tassel

1. Cut one 30" length each red and green 6-strand floss, and two 30" lengths silver blending filament. Carefully separate strands of floss; mix all strands of floss and blending filament, keeping ends even.

2. Wrap length of combined floss and blending filament around 3" cardboard. Cut a 6" length of red floss; slip under loops at one end of cardboard; tie ends tightly in a knot. (Ends will be used to hang tassel from ornament later.)

3. Cut the threads at the other end and remove the tassel from the cardboard. Very carefully, pull apart 6-strand threads. Smooth threads down with fingers or fine comb.

4. Cut 6" length red floss, wrap it around the tassel ½" from looped end and knot it. Thread floss ends in needle and bury thread ends through middle of tassel. Trim tassel evenly to about 2" in length.

Assembly

1. Glue 2½" felt square in center of cardboard square. Glue 2¾" felt square over 2½" square, and 3" white felt square over 2¾" square; this will create a slightly domed top.

2. Trim stitched fabric to a 4" square with stitching

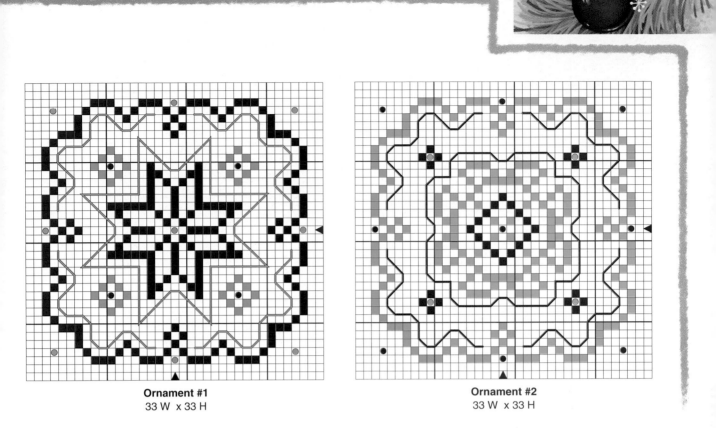

Ornament #1
33 W x 33 H

Ornament #2
33 W x 33 H

COLOR KEY
6-Strand Embroidery Floss
■ Red #321
■ Green #700
✏ Red #321 Backstitch
✏ Green #700 Backstitch
Glass Seed Beads
● Antique red #03049
● Green #02020
Color numbers given are for DMC 6-strand
embroidery floss and Mill Hill glass seed beads.

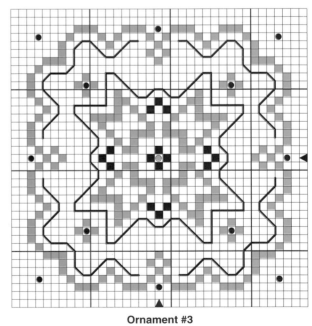

Ornament #3
33 W x 33 H

centered. Center stitched fabric over felt; wrap excess fabric to back and glue to cardboard.

3. Glue red felt square to back to cover raw fabric edges. While glue is still wet, pull felt slightly away from edges so felt does not show from front.

4. Using needle, tie tassel onto ornament corner with floss hanger. Bury floss ends in back between felt and cardboard.

5. Make loop for hanging ornament, using 6 strands red floss and tying to ornament at corner opposite from tassel. ✎

Fabric-Covered Ornaments

Designs by Leslie Hartsock

Materials
Each Ornament

- 6 medium Woodsies wooden diamonds from Forster Inc.
- Fabric scraps: 3 red prints and 3 green prints
- 1 sheet double-sided adhesive
- Pinking shears
- ⅞" wooden button
- 12" gold metallic embroidery floss
- 8" ⅛"-wide green satin ribbon
- 5" square red felt

Precut wooden shapes covered with brightly colored fabric scraps make great ornaments.

Project Note
Refer to photo throughout.

Instructions

1. Cover each wooden diamond with a different fabric scrap: Trace around shape on paper side of adhesive, adding ¼" all around. Cut out around shape; remove paper backing and apply to wrong side of fabric. Cut diamond shape from fabric, trimming corners as needed. Remove second backing sheet from adhesive. Center fabric over wooden diamond and press into place, smoothing excess fabric over edges to back.

2. Using pinking shears and referring to pattern, cut star shape from felt. Glue diamonds to felt in star design, concealing ends of green ribbon behind diamonds for hanging loop. Let dry.

3. Thread metallic gold floss on needle; sew down through button holes, then back up. Tie floss in a bow, trimming ends. Glue button to center of star.

Enlarge pattern 110% to return to original size.

24 • *Quick & Easy Christmas Crafts*

Friendship Ornaments

Designs by Barbara A. Woolley

Materials
Each Ornament

- Brown paper grocery bag
- True Expressions rub-on sayings by Chartpak
- 4 or 5 small buttons
- 7" x 1" frayed strip fabric
- 10" 20-gauge black or aged wire
- Quick Crackle crackle medium from Duncan Enterprises
- Acrylic paints: ivory and burgundy
- Brown wood stain
- Gloss-finish sealer
- Thick tacky glue
- Polyester fiberfill
- Pinking shears or pattern-edge craft scissors
- ¼" round hole punch
- #12 soft, flat paintbrush
- Paper towels
- Iron and ironing board
- Wooden skewer
- Block of plastic foam or craft clay

Each of these heart-shaped ornaments carries a heart-felt message celebrating friendship. Make a set to give to your best friend!

Project Note

Refer to photo throughout for placement.

Instructions

1. Open brown bag; cut out bottom and iron bag flat. Referring to pattern, cut two hearts from paper bag using regular scissors.

2. Glue hearts together along edges, leaving a 1" opening. When glue is completely dry, trim edges of heart with pinking shears or pattern-edge scissors.

3. Place scrap of paper in opening to keep it open; paint both sides of heart with burgundy; let dry. *Note: Insert blunt end of a wooden skewer through opening into heart; stick other end in a piece of plastic foam or craft clay to suspend heart so both sides can dry at once without sticking to work surface.*

4. Paint both sides with crackle medium; let dry.

5. Following manufacturer's instructions, paint both sides of heart with ivory; crackling should start almost immediately. Let dry.

6. Using paper towel, rub a small amount of brown wood stain over both sides of heart; let dry.

7. Following manufacturer's instructions, rub on saying of your choice. Seal heart with gloss sealer; let dry.

8. Remove skewer and scrap of paper from opening. Gently stuff fiberfill about the size of an apple through opening; glue opening closed.

9. Tie frayed fabric strip into a bow; glue bow and buttons to ornament as desired.

10. Punch two holes for hanger through top of heart. Coil wire around paintbrush; slip off paintbrush and thread ends through holes for hanger.

Enlarge pattern 110% to return to original size.

A
n angel's work is never done, and these tin-punch angels are certainly true to form!

Guardian Angels

Designs by Sandra Graham Smith

Materials
- 8" x 10" sheet aluminum flashing
- Masking tape
- Several finishing nails
- Hammer
- Fine-line permanent marking pens: red and black
- Pressed-wood board or other hard protective work surface
- Enamel paints: red, white, black, brown, yellow, green, tan, light blue, pale pink and dark pink
- Yellow dimensional fabric paint
- 6-strand embroidery floss: red and black
- Small needle-nose pliers
- Small piece #16 jack chain
- Tin snips
- Scrap of Spanish moss
- Tacky craft glue
- Small apple charm

Project Notes
Aluminum flashing and #16 jack chain are widely available at hardware stores.

Tan, light blue, pale pink and dark pink paints may be mixed by blending white paint into brown, blue and red paints until desired colors are achieved.

When punching designs, change to a new, sharp nail as needed to maintain holes of an even size.

Patterns are shown in reverse because they are laid on the wrong side of the aluminum flashing to punch designs.

Refer to photo for color placement and details.

Instructions
1. Make paper copies of patterns (page 28); cut out. Trace around paper patterns onto aluminum flashing; cut out shapes with tin snips.

2. Tape paper patterns onto cutout aluminum angels; lay angels on protective work surface. Punch designs using finishing nails and hammer, moving from dot to dot.

3. Remove pattern and tape; turn angels over (smooth side will be back of ornament). Punch hole in one wing where noted for hanger; punch hole in hand and small aluminum rectangle for attaching.

4. Referring to photo and color key (page 28), apply paint inside punched lines, using thick strokes. Let paint dry thoroughly. Paint round, dark pink cheeks on each face and add details to individual designs as follows.

Nurse
1. Using black fine-line marking pen, add round eyes; draw stitching at apron's neck and hem; write "Angel of Mercy" on red skirt. Paint red cross on cap; using red fine-tip marking pen, draw on smile.

2. Paint bandage tray white; let dry. Paint on Band-Aid using brown for center and tan for ends; let dry. Paint tiny air holes on tan portions of Band-Aid with brown paint. Using black fine-line marking pen, write "Band-Aids" on white portion of tray.

3. Attach bandage tray to hand with one chain link. Thread hanging loop of red embroidery floss through hole in wing.

Cook
1. Using black fine-line marking pen, add round eyes; draw stitching at apron's neck and hem; write "An Angel's work is never done!" on light blue skirt. Using red fine-tip marking pen, draw on smile.

2. Paint tan cookies on baking tray; let dry. Add chocolate chips with tiny dots of brown paint.

3. Attach baking tray to hand with one chain link. Thread hanging loop of black embroidery floss through hole in wing.

Teacher
1. Using black fine-line marker, add round eyes; draw stitching at apron's neck and hem; write "Teachers have Class!" on red skirt. Using red marker, draw on smile.

2. Using white paint, write "ABC" on left blackboard wing and "1+2=3" on right blackboard wing. Using yellow dimensional paint, add five dots over top of head for hair.

3. Attach apple charm to hand with one chain link. Thread hanging loop of black embroidery floss through hole in wing.

Gardener
1. Using black marker, add round eyes; draw stitching at apron's neck and hem; write "Guardian Garden Angel" on red skirt. Using red fine-tip marking pen, draw on smile. Glue strands of Spanish moss to head for hair.

2. Paint garden seed packet white; let dry. Add dot of black paint for center of flower; let dry. Add yellow petals; let dry. Add dots of white paint to flower center; using black fine-line marking pen, write "Flower Seeds" on packet and add detail lines to yellow petals.

3. Attach seed packet to hand with one chain link. Thread hanging loop of red embroidery floss through hole in wing.

Gardener Angel

Cooking Angel

Nurse Angel

Cookie Sheet
Flower Seeds
Band-Aids
Cut 1 for each

Teacher Angel

Folk-Art Ornaments
instructions begin
on page 30

*T*urn your assorted scrap-bag remnants into two Christmas treasures with these easy-to-make ornaments with a pleasant folk-art look!

Folk-Art Ornaments

Designs by Chris Malone • shown on page 29

Materials

Mitten

- 2" x 3½" piece red wool fabric
- 3 (⅝"–¾") white buttons
- 1¾" natural-color crocheted flower from Wimpole Street Creations' Miniature Crochet Assortment

Stocking

- 2" x 3½" piece dark green wool fabric
- 3 (⁷⁄₁₆"–⁹⁄₁₆") red buttons
- Dark green 6-strand cotton embroidery floss
- 1" and 1½" natural-color crocheted flowers from Wimpole Street Creations' Miniature Crochet Assortment
- 1½" ⅛"-diameter twig

Each Ornament

- 8" square Warm & Natural Needled Cotton from Warm Products, Inc.
- 2" x 3½" piece fusible webbing
- 6-strand embroidery floss: taupe and white
- 10" ⅜"-diameter natural-color cord
- Craft glue

Project Notes

Separate 6-strand embroidery floss into individual plies, then recombine the correct number to be used for stitching without twisting. Refer to photograph (page 29) throughout for placement and stitching details.

Mitten

1. Referring to patterns throughout, cut two mittens from needled batting.

2. Following manufacturer's instructions, fuse webbing to wrong side of red wool fabric. Trace one heart onto paper backing; cut out. Peel off paper backing and fuse heart to front of one mitten.

3. Using 2 plies white embroidery floss, backstitch "Joy" on heart and blanket-stitch around heart.

4. Using 3 plies embroidery floss, attach one button to heart and others to mitten as shown by sewing through button holes and tying ends in knots on top of buttons; trim ends to ½".

5. Pin mittens together, wrong sides facing. Using 3 plies taupe embroidery floss, blanket-stitch mittens together, stitching over only the single front edge at top of mitten so mitten is open.

6. For hanging loop, fold ⅜"-diameter cord in half; insert 1" of one end into opening on one side of mitten. Blind-stitch or glue in place. Repeat with other end on other side of mitten opening.

7. Glue or stitch crocheted flower at top of mitten.

Stocking

1. Cut two stocking shapes from needled batting.

2. Following manufacturer's instructions, fuse webbing to wrong side of dark green wool fabric. Trace tree onto paper backing; cut out. Peel off paper backing and fuse tree to front of one stocking.

3. Using 2 plies white embroidery floss, blanket-stitch around tree.

4. Using 3 plies dark green embroidery floss, attach buttons to tree by sewing through button holes and tying ends in knots on top of buttons; trim ends to ½".

5. Apply a thin line of glue to one side of twig; glue to stocking below tree for tree trunk. Using 3 plies taupe embroidery floss, make stitch near top of twig; tie ends in knot over twig and trim ends to ½". Repeat near bottom of twig.

6. Using 2 plies dark green embroidery floss, backstitch "Noel" at bottom of stocking.

7. Pin stocking pieces together, wrong sides facing. Using 3 plies taupe embroidery floss, blanket-stitch stockings together, stitching over only the single front edge at top of stocking so stocking is open.

8. For hanging loop, fold ⅜"-diameter cord in half; insert 1" of one end into opening on one side of stocking. Blind-stitch or glue in place. Repeat with other end on other side of stocking opening.

9. Glue or stitch 1½" crocheted flower at top corner; glue or stitch 1" flower beside twig.

Instructions

1. Referring to patterns, cut two mittens from checks paper, reversing one, and two trees from mini dot paper, reversing one. Tear remaining paper into six 1" pieces for patches.

2. Mix water with all colors of paint to make them transparent. Paint mitten cuff with dark forest green. Paint two patches maroon, two leprechaun green and two Prussian blue. Let dry.

3. Referring to photo, glue one patch of each color to front of mitten and tree. Let glue dry.

4. Using 6-strand embroidery floss, sew primitive cross-stitches around patches on mitten and tree. Sew or glue green button to tree and red button to mitten.

5. Sew halves of trees and mittens together with a running stitch, wrong sides facing, stuffing ornaments with fiberfill as you sew.

6. Tie two four-strand bows from natural raffia; glue one to each ornament. Fold jute pieces in half to form loops; knot ends. Glue knots to backs of ornaments. Let glue dry.

T his duo of charming country ornaments can be made in a snap with scraps of craft paper, a couple of buttons, twine and raffia!

Paper-Craft Ornaments

Designs by
Deborah Spofford

Materials

- 6" x 12" Paperbilities embossed kraft mini-dot paper from MPR Associates, Inc.
- 5" x 10" Paperbilities embossed kraft checks paper from MPR Associates, Inc.
- Acrylic paints: leprechaun green, maroon, Prussian blue and dark forest green
- #4 shader paintbrush
- 8 (12") strands natural raffia
- 2 (10") strands natural jute
- Green 6-strand embroidery floss
- Needle
- ½" buttons: red and green
- Polyester fiberfill
- Tacky craft glue

Turn those ugly old neckties into a little touch of heaven with these adorable angel ornaments! They're sure to delight the man of the house!

Necktie Angels

Designs by Delores Ruzicka

Materials
Each Ornament

- 3" x 5" piece ⅛"-thick birch plywood
- Band saw or scroll saw
- Sandpaper
- Drill and ¹⁄₁₆" wood bit
- 5" piece cut from the skinny end of man's necktie
- Acrylic paints: blush, medium red, medium apricot and ivory
- ½" paintbrush
- 1" wooden round ball with ¼" hole
- 4" ¼"-diameter wooden dowel
- 1½" wooden star cutout
- Black fine-line permanent marking pen
- Light brown Lil Loopies doll hair from One & Only Creations
- 10" ⅛"-wide satin ribbon in coordinating color
- 11" stovepipe wire
- 1" gold ring
- Crafty Magic Melt hot-glue gun and wood-glue sticks from Adhesive Technologies, Inc.

Instructions

1. Referring to pattern, trace wings onto plywood; cut out and sand edges. Drill holes where indicated.

2. Paint sides and edges of wings with ivory paint; let dry. Using fine-line marking pen, draw dot-dash pattern around outer edges of wings.

3. Glue ball to one end of dowel. Paint ball with blush paint, using two coats if necessary; let dry. Referring to Face-Painting Diagram, add cheeks by dipping your little finger into a drop of medium red paint; touch fingertip to ball; let dry. Using fine-line marking pen, draw two oval eyes with eyelashes; add ivory highlight dots to cheeks and eyes.

4. Glue dowel stick inside necktie, lightly gathering tie around neck area. Glue wings to back of tie.

5. Glue doll hair to angel's head in desired style; glue on gold ring for halo. Tie ribbon in small bow with long streamers; glue under doll's chin.

6. Paint star with medium apricot; let dry. With fine-line marking pen, draw dot-dash pattern around edge. Glue star to front of angel.

7. Wrap wire around pencil; pull wire to desired length and attach ends through holes in wings.

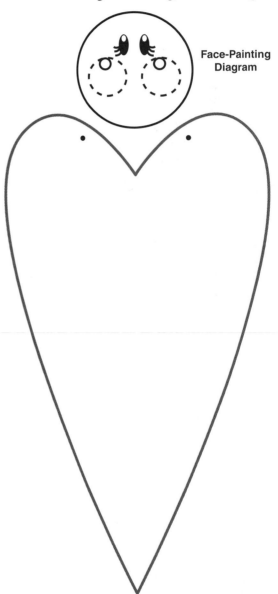

Face-Painting Diagram

Wear It Christmas

Clothing, Jewelry & More!

There are special people who live, eat and breathe Christmas from around Nov. 1 until Jan. 1. They do their very best to spread Christmas cheer to everyone they meet. Whether you're one of those exceptionally festive folks or not, this chapter of delightful wearables—including vests, sweatshirts, pins, jewelry and more—will make this Christmas one of the merriest ever! So, spread that Christmas cheer around by proudly wearing it!

Pattern Note
Refer to photo throughout.

Instructions

1. Wash sweatshirt in warm water to remove sizing; *do not use fabric softener.* When shirt is dry, slip over painting board or other sturdy cardboard and secure with pins as needed so surface to be decorated is flat and smooth.

2. Peel printed liner (side with words) from fusible web and adhere sticky side to backs of fabrics. Referring to patterns, cut trees and star from fused fabrics: cut seven large trees from green print A and one from Christmas print; cut 10 medium trees from green print B; cut 10 small trees from green print C; cut one star from yellow fabric.

3. Peel paper from backs of trees and arrange on sweatshirt as desired. Appliqués may be repositioned until they are ironed in place. On sample, small trees are arranged first, nearest the neck, then the medium trees, and then the large trees, with the front center space reserved for the large tree cut from Christmas print. Six small trees, four medium trees and four large trees, plus the Christmas tree with the yellow star on top, are arranged on the front of the shirt; the remaining trees are arranged on the back.

4. When you have achieved desired arrangement, cover with damp pressing cloth and, with heated iron, press in place for about 10 seconds using continuous steam. Move to next area and repeat the process, overlapping

S pend an evening trimming your tree after trimming this country Christmas sweatshirt! Various green prints, assorted buttons and paints really make a right jolly top.

O Tannenbaum Sweatshirt

Design by Barbara A. Woolley

Materials

- Natural-color sweatshirt
- Fabric:
  ¼ yard each of 3 coordinating green plaids, checks or prints
  10" x 5" piece bright Christmas print or plaid
  2" square bright yellow
- 1 yard Steam-a-Seam 2 double-sided iron-on fusible web
- 6-strand embroidery floss: bright red and bright green
- Approximately 12 small white and cream 2-hole and 4-hole buttons
- Dimensional fabric paint: red, black and silver glitter
- T-shirt painting board or large piece of sturdy cardboard covered with plastic wrap
- Pins
- Steam iron
- Pressing cloth

ironed areas, until all areas are fused in place.

5. Outline all trees using black dimensional paint (this will help secure appliqués to shirt). Let dry.

6. Tie knots through buttons with red and green floss so that floss ends protrude from front; clip floss ends to about ¼" and fray. Using matching floss, sew buttons randomly to Christmas tree.

7. Using silver glitter dimensional paint, add stars around treetops at neck. Using red dimensional paint, write "Happy Holidays" on shirt front.

Design by Angie Wilhite

W atch your little one's eyes light up when you give her this adorable Christmas vest! Adorned with a Santa, sweetheart Christmas tree and blue star buttons, this vest will delight everyone young and old alike!

The Littlest Christmas Vest

Design by Angie Wilhite

Materials

- Child's white felt vest
- Rainbow Classic Felt from Kunin Felt:
  8" x 10" piece cranberry
  6" square kelly green
  3" square cashmere tan
- 4" x 5" piece antique white Rainbow Plush Felt from Kunin Felt
- Small Faces for Places #PT 10005 face button from True Colors International
- ¼ yard Therm O Web HeatnBond Lite iron-on adhesive
- ¼ yard Therm O Web pressing paper
- DMC rayon embroidery floss:
  Cream #30746
  Black #30310
- 3 blue star buttons #4260 from Blumenthal Lansing Co.
- Matching blue embroidery floss or thread

Pattern Note

Refer to photo throughout.

Instructions

1. Following manufacturer's instructions, apply iron-on adhesive to wrong side of cranberry, kelly green, cashmere tan and antique white plush felt. Referring to patterns (page 39), cut Santa's robe, sleeves, hat and heart for tree from cranberry; cut Santa's hat brim and beard from antique white plush; cut tree trunk from cashmere tan and tree from

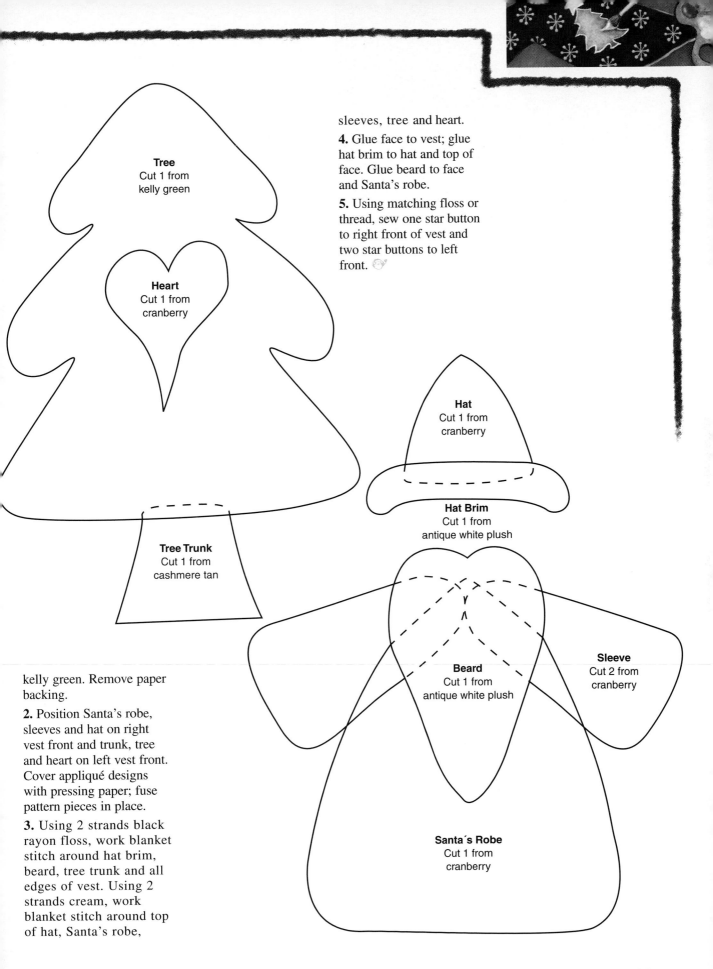

Tree
Cut 1 from
kelly green

Heart
Cut 1 from
cranberry

Tree Trunk
Cut 1 from
cashmere tan

sleeves, tree and heart.

4. Glue face to vest; glue hat brim to hat and top of face. Glue beard to face and Santa's robe.

5. Using matching floss or thread, sew one star button to right front of vest and two star buttons to left front.

Hat
Cut 1 from
cranberry

Hat Brim
Cut 1 from
antique white plush

Beard
Cut 1 from
antique white plush

Sleeve
Cut 2 from
cranberry

Santa´s Robe
Cut 1 from
cranberry

kelly green. Remove paper backing.

2. Position Santa's robe, sleeves and hat on right vest front and trunk, tree and heart on left vest front. Cover appliqué designs with pressing paper; fuse pattern pieces in place.

3. Using 2 strands black rayon floss, work blanket stitch around hat brim, beard, tree trunk and all edges of vest. Using 2 strands cream, work blanket stitch around top of hat, Santa's robe,

*B*arely peeking over the top of his monstrous mustache and beard, this hand-painted Santa pin will help you wish your friends a ho-ho-ho happy holiday!

Spectacled Santa

Design by Paula Bales

Materials
- 3" x 4" piece of ³⁄₁₆"-thick basswood from Midwest Products
- Americana acrylic paints from DecoArt:
  Santa red #DA170
  Sand #DA4
  Mocha #DA60
- Oak gel stain from DecoArt
- Tulip black slick paint
- #8 shader paintbrush #7300 from Loew-Cornell
- Toothpick or wooden skewer
- Black fine-point permanent marking pen
- Cotton muslin
- Scroll saw
- Fine sandpaper
- Natural jute
- 22-gauge wire
- ¼"-diameter wooden dowel
- 1" pin back
- Hot-glue gun

Project Note
Refer to photo throughout.

Painting Santa
1. Trace pattern onto wood; cut out with scroll saw. Sand edges until smooth. Wipe off sawdust.

2. Stain wooden cutout with gel stain following manufacturer's instructions; let dry completely.

3. Paint hat area with Santa red and face with mocha; let dry.

4. Dilute a small amount of Santa red with a little water; paint cheeks with this mixture; let dry.

5. Using tip of paintbrush handle or blunt end of wooden skewer, dot on eyes with black slick paint. Let dry. Add eye highlights by dotting tiny spots of sand paint onto eyes using toothpick or point of wooden skewer. Let dry.

6. Using black fine-point permanent marker, outline hat and add eyebrows and "crow's-feet."

Muslin Beard
1. Tear muslin into 3" x ½" strips; glue to face for beard.

2. Tear two 6" x ½" strips muslin; knot together in center for nose and mustache; glue to Santa's face.

3. If desired, give Santa's beard a more rumpled look by wetting hand and randomly squeezing muslin strips to wrinkle fabric; let dry undisturbed.

4. Trim beard as desired.

Finishing & Assembly
1. Tear ¾"-wide strip muslin; glue at base of hat for trim. Glue small pieces of muslin at tip of hat for "pompom."

2. Make glasses by wrapping wire around dowel; remove dowel and wrap a second circle next to the first. Trim excess wire and glue glasses above Santa's nose.

3. Tie jute into small bow; glue to muslin trim on hat.

4. Glue pin back to back of Santa.

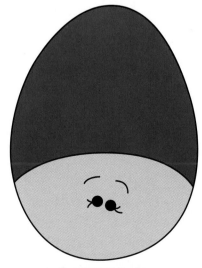

Spectacled Santa

*D*ecorate your wristwatch with this adorable frosty couple. Although a small part of your outfit, this little addition will capture the attention and compliments of many!

Watch It Snow

Design by Sandy Laipply

Materials

- *Wood ring round wristwatch from Wizards of Wood*
- *Ceramcoat acrylic paints by Delta Technical Coatings, Inc.:*
  Wedgwood blue #02-069
  Liberty blue #02-416
  Opaque red #02-507
  White #02-505
  Black #02-506
- *Water-base varnish from Delta Technical Coatings, Inc.*
- *Silver Brush Limited paintbrushes from Golden Natural:*
  Angular ⅛" Series #2006-S
  Liner #2/0 Series #2005-S
  Bright #4 Series #2002-S
- *Transfer paper*
- *Stylus*
- *Fine sandpaper*

Watch It Snow

Instructions

1. Following manufacturer's instructions, prepare watch for painting. Gently sand wood; wipe off dust and seal with a coat of water-base varnish. Let dry completely.

2. Trace pattern onto tracing paper; cut out circle. Cut small piece of transfer paper in circle of the same size. Place transfer paper atop watch, then pattern atop transfer paper. With stylus, trace pattern. Remove pattern and transfer paper.

3. Base-coat snow people and ground white; base-coat sky with liberty blue. Base-coat snowman's hat with black and snow lady's hat with opaque red.

4. Paint scarf and bow opaque red.

5. Using angular brush, shade snow people with Wedgwood blue. Paint "hills" in snow with Wedgwood blue.

6. Highlight snowman's hat with white. Mix equal amounts opaque red and black; use mixture to shade snow lady's hat and bow.

7. Thin a small amount of white paint with water; using liner brush, paint snowflakes in the sky with thinned mixture.

8. Using stylus dipped in black, dot on eyes and buttons.

9. When all paint is completely dry, apply three coats of water-base varnish to painted surface, allowing each coat to dry and sanding lightly between coats.

Christmas Confections Jacket

Decidedly delicious, this jacket will make a sweet gift for a special person on your gift list. You may want to wear it yourself as a hostess jacket, or when you deliver Christmas goodies to your neighbors and friends.

Christmas Confections Jacket

Design by Charlyne Stewart

Materials

- Simple jacket pattern (see Project Note)
- Appropriate yardage of red fleece to make jacket (see Project Note)
- Appropriate yardage of red, white and green striped fabric for binding (see Project Note)
- ⅛ yard brown fleece
- ⅛ yard red print fabric
- ⅛ yard red-and-white striped fabric
- ⅛ yard brown-gold print fabric
- ⅛ yard green print fabric
- ⅛ yard white print fabric
- ⅝ yard Wonder Under fusible web
- Package small iridescent pink sequins
- Package crystal seed beads
- Spool sewing threads: white, red, green, brown and brown gold, to match fabrics
- Pressing cloth
- Steam iron
- Sewing machine with open-toe foot

Project Note

McCall's pattern #8862 was used for sample; only front, back and sleeve pieces were used. Sample required 1⅝ yards red fleece and ¾ yard striped fabric for binding and ties.

Appliqués & Jacket

1. Referring to patterns (pages 42–44), trace three gingerbread men, five candy canes, three chocolate drops, five wrapped candies and three cupcakes onto smooth side of fusible web; for round peppermint candies, trace 10 circles and 10 swirl sections onto smooth side of fusible web. Cut out; cut cupcake shapes apart into cupcake bases, iced tops and cherries.

2. Following manufacturer's instructions, fuse each piece to wrong side of fabric: fuse gingerbread men and chocolate drops to brown fleece; fuse candy canes to red-and-white striped fabric; fuse cupcake bases to brown-gold print; fuse cupcake iced tops, five peppermint circles and five peppermint swirls to white print; fuse cupcake cherries, wrapped candies and five peppermint swirls to green print; fuse five peppermint circles to red print.

3. From red fleece cut jacket fronts, back and sleeves, using commercial pattern pieces. Referring to pocket pattern (page 44), cut two pockets from red fleece.

4. Referring to photo throughout, position confections on jacket fronts and pockets, allowing for ⅜" seams on pockets. Peel off paper backing and, using a pressing cloth, fuse confections in place, following

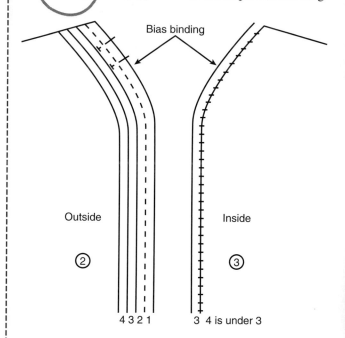

Bias binding

Outside

②

4 3 2 1

Inside

③

3 4 is under 3

Binding Diagram

1 Press bias strips in half lengthwise. Open and press each side to meet in the center (four sections).

② Facing right sides together, pin bias strip along the edge and stitch on the first creased line.

③ Fold binding to the garment back and slipstitch.

There are two layers of the binding on the outside and two on the inside.

manufacturer's instructions. For swirl candies, fuse circles in place first;

then fuse green swirls to white circles and white swirls to red circles.

5. Attach open-toe foot to sewing machine; set machine for narrow, slightly open zigzag stitch. Using matching threads, machine-appliqué around each confection. Increase width of zigzag stitch slightly; machine-appliqué around all pieces again.

6. Referring to pattern for placement, attach eyes, mouth and buttons to gingerbread men: Thread needle with white thread; come up from underside of garment; thread on sequin, then bead, and go back down through sequin; knot thread ends to secure.

7. Following pattern instructions, sew jacket fronts to back and sew in sleeves; hem jacket bottom. Seam finishing is optional for fleece fabric.

Binding & Finishing

1. Measure edges of sleeve hems, pocket tops and front opening in jacket, including neck area. From striped binding fabric, cut binding on the bias, 2½" wide by the length measured plus sufficient seam allowance for turning under ends. Use the longest strips possible, piecing as necessary.

2. Fold binding strips in half down their length, wrong sides facing; press. Open seam and fold each half to meet in center; press again.

3. Lay prepared binding over edge of fabric; pin in place and slipstitch by hand,

Continued on next page

using matching thread.

4. Using matching thread, hand-stitch pockets to jacket fronts.

5. Cut two 10" binding strips for jacket ties. Fold under edges on one piece as for binding; stitch open edge and both ends closed to make tie. Repeat with other strip.

6. Stitch ties to jacket front as shown on photo. Knot each tie 1" from end.

Escort your special Santa to this year's Christmas gathering. Adorned with our holly necklace and matching earrings, your bells will be a-jingling.

Jingle Bell Jewelry

Designs by Barbara A. Woolley

Materials

- Jingle bells: 4 (¾"), 2 (1") and 1 (1¼")
- 45" #2 red rat-tail cord
- 14 (½"-wide) red satin ribbon bows
- 7 (8mm) gold jump rings
- 2 fishhook earring ear wires
- 20mm wooden beads:
  10 green
  4 white
  4 red
- Ceramcoat Decorative Snow artificial snow paste from Delta Technical Coatings, Inc.
- Delta Shiny Liner dimensional paint from Delta Technical Coatings, Inc.: red and green
- Satin-finish white spray paint
- Very fine-tip permanent black marking pen
- Wooden toothpicks
- White craft glue
- Needle-nose pliers

Project Note

Refer to photo throughout.

Jingle Bells

1. Spray all jingle bells with white spray paint; let dry.

2. Using needle-nose pliers, attach jump ring to each jingle bell.

3. Referring to photo, paint clusters of holly leaves and berries on each jingle bell using red and green dimensional paints. Holly usually has clusters of three leaves and three berries. When paint is completely dry, add veins to leaves using black marking pen.

4. Using toothpick, apply a small "drift" of snow to top of each jingle bell. Press two bows into top of each jingle bell while snow is still wet. Set aside to dry thoroughly.

Necklace Assembly

1. Find center of rat-tail cord; tie a simple overhand knot. Thread 1¼" jingle bell onto cord and slide to knot; tie another knot to secure jingle bell in center of cord.

2. Thread bells and beads onto one side of cord and knot as follows: green bead, white bead, red bead, knot; 1" jingle bell, knot; green bead, white bead, red bead, knot; ¾" jingle bell, knot; two green beads; knot. Secure another single green bead at very end of cord between two knots.

3. Repeat step 2 for other side of necklace.

Earrings

Using needle-nose pliers, carefully open hanging loop on ear wire. Slide jump ring of ¾" jingle bell onto loop. Close loop carefully and securely with needle-nose pliers. Repeat for second earring. ✆

Bedazzle an ordinary black dress by adding ribbons, roses and radiant stars. What a festive appearance mother and daughter will make at a family holiday gathering!

Elegant Christmas Combo

Designs by Judi Kauffman

Materials
Both Dresses

- Bucilla 100-percent silk ribbon:
  2 packages 4mm-wide light coral #531
  1 package 13mm-wide variegated bright greens #1301
  2 packages 13mm-wide variegated burgundies #1306
  1 package 13mm-wide variegated mint greens #1309
  4 packages 13mm-wide variegated olive greens #1311
  3 packages 13mm-wide variegated Christmas reds #1315
- #10 millener's needle
- Chenille needle
- Small gold star sequins
- Gold seed beads
- Coordinating sewing threads: olive and dark red

Project Note
Refer to photos throughout.

Instructions
1. Using tailor's chalk, draw a swag across neckline of dress to resemble Christmas garland.

2. Thread two needles with olive sewing thread; one will be used for gathering and the other for sewing. Following instructions for ruching, gather variegated olive ribbon, sewing it in place along marked swag line as you gather.

3. Following instructions for gathered roses and using dark red sewing thread, make rosettes for clusters from Christmas red and burgundy variegated ribbons. Each cluster on adult's garment includes three roses; each cluster on child's garment includes two. Set roses aside.

4. Following instructions for shawl collar leaves, make two leaves for each gathered rose, using variegated olive, mint green and bright green ribbons.

5. Sew rose clusters at high points of garland (Fig. 1). Tucking leaves under roses so cut ends are hidden, sew leaves in place.

6. Using variegated Christmas red and burgundy ribbons, make French knot clusters along the garland (one to three knots at intervals), varying colors as you like. Top each 13mm ribbon knot with a French knot of 4mm light coral ribbon so they look like flowers.

7. Swirl light coral ribbon around and through garland, leaving it very loose and dimensional. Tie bows wherever you like. Bring bow tails to inside of garment and secure with a knot.

8. Sew star sequins along the garland as desired, threading sequin onto needle from back to front, then threading on gold seed bead; go back down through star sequin and secure to garment, knotting thread on back. ✂

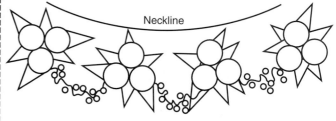

Elegant Christmas Combo
Fig. 1

RUCHING

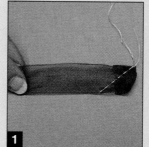

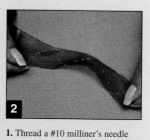

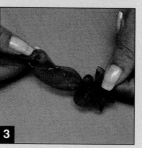

1. Thread a #10 milliner's needle with thread to match the ribbon (we're showing a contrast so you can see). Turn the raw edge of the ribbon under at the beginning.

2. Stitch angled lines of running stitches. Catch the edge of the ribbon each time you change angle.

3. After three or four inches, use the thread to gather the ribbon. Continue o zig and zag, gather and adjust. For a very long ruched ribbon, sew it onto your project as you go (every four inches) to keep it from twisting.

Step-by-step photos for silk ribbon embroidery are provided courtesy of Bucilla from Fifty Fabulous Stitches—Silk Ribbon Embroidery Encyclopedia by Judi Kauffman. The volume is available from your local craft retailer, or from Sugarloaf Craft Co. for $4.99 plus s&h (see Shopper's Guide, page 175).

GATHERED ROSETTE or FREEFORM FLOWER

3. Gather to form a bud. Secure with a stitch or two at base.

4. Continue to make running stitches, two or three inches at a time, gathering the ribbon while you twirl it around itself. Secure at the base as you go. The longer the ribbon, the fuller the flower. Make the last few running stitches cross the end of the ribbon at the angle to form a petal.

SHAWL COLLAR LEAF AND PETAL

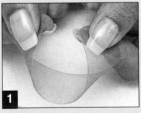

1. For petals and leaves that end in a point, fold a piece of ribbon at an angle like a shawl collar.

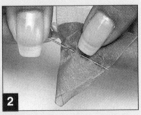

2. With matching sewing thread (we're showing a contrast so you can see), sew a running stitch line across the base.

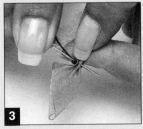

3. Gather the petal, tie off the thread, and cut off excess ribbon.

4. Sew in place.

5. Hide the raw edge under a button, bead or flower

1. Thread a needle with sewing thread to match the ribbon. Fold one end of the ribbon down at an angle leaving a tail to use as a handle.

2. Fold the ribbon back across itself. Stitch three or four running stitches along the bottom edge.

5. Stitch several times so the flower can't pull out. Cut off excess ribbon.

6. Sew the rosette to your project. If your project uses a lot of rosettes it's a good idea to make them all first and sew them on later. Then you can move them around till they look just right.

Keep spills off your little one by donning him or her in this adorable bib. Your little one will look as cute as a button in photos of his or her very first Christmas!

Ho-Ho-Ho Baby Bib

Design by Nancy Hearne

Materials

- *Preprinted Velour Baby Bib with Santa-and-Snowman pattern from Charles Craft*
- *DMC 6-strand embroidery floss as listed in color key*
- *#24 tapestry needle*
- *DMC Cebelia 50-gram ball white crochet cotton size 30*
- *Size 12 steel crochet hook*

Project Note

Chart shows part of complete design. Stitch design beginning at left edge of chart and left edge of bib. Continue design as needed to stitch across bib.

Cross-Stitch

1. Using 2 strands floss, cross-stitch design onto even-weave portion of bib.
2. Using 1 strand of gray floss, backstitch around hatbands and pompoms on Santa hats.

Crocheted Trim

Add crocheted trim across top and bottom of even-weave strip.

Row 1 (RS): Attach cotton in bib, ch 5 (counts as first hdc, ch 3), sk 2 squares of fabric, hdc around next square of fabric, *ch 3, sk 2 squares of fabric, hdc around next square of fabric, rep from * across, turn.

Row 2: Sl st into ch-3 sp, ch 3, [work 2 dc holding last lp of each on hook, yo and through all lps on hook] in same ch-3 sp, *ch 3, in next ch-3 sp work 3-dc cl (work 3 dc holding last lp of each on hook, yo and pull through all lps on hook), rep from * across, turn.

Row 3: Sl st into ch-3 sp, ch 1, 3 sc in same ch-3 sp, *ch 3, 3 sc in next sp, rep from * across, fasten off.

COLOR KEY

6-Strand Embroidery Floss
☐ White
■ Bright Christmas red #816
▨ Christmas green #3818
☐ Old gold #3820
✏ Gray #712 Backstitch
Color numbers are given for DMC 6-Strand Embroidery Floss.

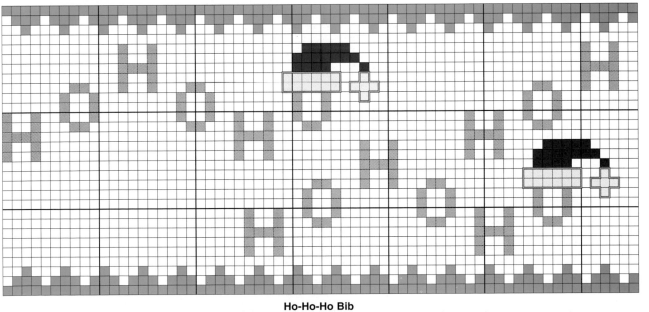

Ho-Ho-Ho Bib
Position left edge of design on left edge of bib and continue design as needed to fill stitching area

Embroider an ordinary vest and give it an extra-ordinary look perfect for a casual or elegant holiday or New Year's celebration!

Glittery Vest

Design by Victoria Adams Brown, courtesy of Kreinik Manufacturing

Materials

- Denim vest
- Pink water-soluble marking pen
- Chenille needles: #18, #20 and #22
- Kreinik ⅛" Ribbon:
  Pink #007
  Light purple #012
  Purple #012HL
  Hot pink #024
- Green #008 Kreinik Medium (#16) Braid
- Kreinik Fine (#8) Braid:
  Gold #002
  Kelly green #015
- Cotton swab

Project Notes

Refer to photo and Stitch Diagrams throughout.

Work with 16" lengths of ribbon and braid, knotting one end to secure them to fabric.

Instructions

1. Wash and dry vest. Referring to photo, sketch design on each side of vest using water-soluble marking pen.

2. Make spokes for spiderweb roses using gold fine (#8) braid, placing roses as desired. Complete roses using assorted colors of ⅛" ribbon.

3. Using kelly green fine (#8) braid, work stem stitch tendrils.

4. Using green medium (#16) braid, work leaf stitch leaves around spiderweb roses.

5. Using purple and pink ⅛" ribbons, work lazy-daisy petals of daisies. Using gold fine (#8) braid, add three two-wrap French knots to center of each daisy.

6. Stitch a cascade of hot pink ⅛" ribbon through floral design, beginning at top on one side of vest: Bring ribbon through to front, twist ribbon once, and go down vest front, executing a 1" twisted straight stitch. Bring needle to front of fabric and make a one-wrap French knot. Continue the cascade of ribbon to end of design, keeping ribbon loose. Repeat on other side of vest.

7. Remove any remaining visible marks from marking pen by touching marks with a wet cotton swab. ✂

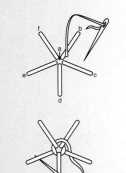

Leaf Stitch

Complete a vertical straight stitch to start. Then, come up at A. Push needle down at B and back up at C, keeping braid under the needle and allowing it to drape. To hold the draped braid in place, go down on the other side of braid near C, forming a straight stitch across braid. One leaf stitch is shown completed under the vertical straight stitch. Completed series of stitches forming leaf is also shown. These stitches may be done with space between as shown, or close to each other to completely cover fabric.

Stem Stitch

Working from left to right, make slightly slanting stitches along the line of the stem: Bring braid up at A and down at B, then up at C, half the length of the stitch beyond B. Continue in same manner, bringing needle up in middle of previous stitch.

Spiderweb Rose

To make spokes, come up at A, then down at B, up at A, down at C, etc., making five spokes. Thread tapestry needle with ribbon and come up at center as shown. Begin weaving over one spoke and under the next, etc., around and around the center; let ribbon twist to give it a natural look. Keep ribbon snug for the first few rounds, then allow it to loosen a bit. Continue weaving over and under, around and around, until spokes are completely covered.

Lazy-Daisy Stitch

Bring ribbon up at A and down at B (notice that A and B are almost the same hole, but not quite). Leave a loop the size of petal you want; come up at C and down at D. Repeat for additional petals.

French Knot

Come up through fabric and wrap braid (or ribbon) as directed around needle. Hold braid to the side and snug the braid up against the needle down by the fabric. Insert needle down right next to where you came up. Keep tension on braid while pulling needle through fabric to keep braid from knotting.

Warm up after a romp in the new-fallen snow by donning these whimsical sweatshirts, one for Mom or Dad and one for a child. Your love of the winter wonderland will be evident to those who see your happy, hand-painted shirt.

Project Notes

Refer to photos throughout.

Use a relatively dry brush for painting. Rinse thoroughly between colors, and dry well with paper towels.

All shading is done by loading the brush with gel medium, then side-loading the paint with a *tiny* amount of paint on one side. Stroke the brush on the palette several times so that the paint moves across the brush in a fading manner. Paints may be thinned with the gel medium. Avoid adding water to the paints as this may cause the paints to bleed when applied to fabric.

If paint is accidentally applied to unwanted areas, *let dry,* then remove by gently scrubbing with alcohol-soaked cotton swabs.

Preparation

1. Launder sweatshirts in warm water using a mild detergent but *no fabric softener.* Make sure all soapsuds are rinsed out of garment; run through rinse cycle twice, if necessary. Tumble-dry until damp, then hang to dry. Turn right side out and press any wrinkles.

2. Insert T-shirt painting board into sweatshirt. To keep shirt from shifting while painting, pin sides and top of shirt front and back together close to painting board; pin together any fabric extending beyond bottom of painting board. Shirt should lie flat with a seam of pins surrounding the edge of the shirt board.

3. Trace pattern (pages 54–55) onto tracing paper with a pencil; turn traced pattern over and trace design on backside with tailor's chalk.

4. Center traced pattern on shirt front, chalk side down. Secure with one piece tape. Using stylus or craft stick, trace over pattern lines *except* facial details, holly and jingle bells.

Painting Snowman

Santa

1. Use #4 and #10 shaders and white paint to paint snowman Santa, snow piles and snowballs. Referring to Project Note, using robin blue, shade Santa where head snowball rests on center snowball, where center rests on bottom, and where coat, hat and mittens overlap body. Also shade all snow piles and snowballs where they overlap.

2. Using #6 shader and holly day red, paint Santa's coat and hat. Using #10

Snow Characters Sweatshirts

Designs by Debbie Williams

Materials

- Adult- and child-size navy blue sweatshirts, at least 50 percent cotton
- Starlite Shimmering Fabric Color from Delta Technical Coatings, Inc.:
  Gold #10-402-0101
  Kelly #10-404-0101
  Robin blue #10-4090101
  Starlite white #10-420-0101
  Deep clover #10-421-0101
  Charcoal #10-424-0101
  Holly day red #10-431-0101
- Pigskin #10-325-0101 Brush-On Fabric Color from Delta Technical Coatings, Inc.
- Starlite Glitter Fabric Color from Delta Technical Coatings, Inc.:
  Crystal ice #10-501-0101
  Sparkling silver #10-503-0101
- Fabric Gel Fabric Medium from Delta Technical Coatings, Inc.
- Fashion Show 20mm Fine Line Writer Tip from Plaid Enterprises, Inc.
- La Corneille-Golden Taklon paintbrushes from Loew-Cornell:
  Shaders #7300-10, #7300-6 and #7300-4
  Liner #7350-1
  ⅛" deerfoot stippler #7850
- Double-end stylus #DES from Loew-Cornell
- Blue Super Chacopaper transfer paper from Loew-Cornell
- T-shirt painting boards or large pieces of sturdy cardboard covered with plastic wrap
- Cellophane tape
- Straight pins
- Iron
- White tailor's chalk

4. Using white and ⅛" deerfoot stippler, stipple fur trim on coat. Do not cover sweatshirt fabric completely with paint; color of sweatshirt gives texture to the fur. When all fur is stippled and dry, stipple charcoal onto areas where fur is overlapped.

5. Transfer facial details and holly to snowman with transfer paper.

coal, paint eyes, eyelashes and mouth. Using handle of liner brush, paint nose with holly day red. Using smaller end of stylus and white, dot highlights onto eyes.

8. Using #10 shader and gold fabric color, paint moon.

Painting Snowman Reindeer

1. Use #4 and #10 shaders and white paint to paint snowman reindeer, snow piles and snowballs. Referring to Project Note, using robin blue, shade reindeer where top of head snowball rests on muzzle,

Snow Character
Large Sweatshirt
Using photo as a guide, reposition elements as on original.

shader and charcoal, shade overlapped areas and creases in coat and hat.

3. Using #4 shader and kelly, paint Santa's mittens. Using #6 shader and deep clover, shade thumb creases in mittens and overlapped areas. (Some touch-up work may be needed on mittens after fur trim is painted.)

6. Using liner and kelly, paint holly leaves onto collar. Outline upper edge of top holly leaf with deep clover to separate leaves. Add berries with stylus tip dipped in holly day red.

7. Shade Santa's cheeks with #6 shader and robin blue. Using liner and char-

at base of muzzle, and where wreath collar overlaps snow body. Also shade all snow piles and snowballs where they overlap.

2. Using the liner, paint reindeer's antlers with pigskin. When dry, add bits

of snow to antlers with white.

3. Using #4 shader and kelly, paint wreath collar. While paint is wet, load ⅛" deerfoot stippler with kelly and stipple side and bottom edges to create a looser greenery look. When dry, use #10 shader and deep clover to shade top edge. Also, lightly stipple deep clover over remainder of wreath; let dry.

4. Transfer facial details onto head and jingle bells pattern onto wreath collar with transfer paper. Using #4 shader, paint bells with pigskin (or paint by making dots with the end of a large brush handle). Let dry. Using liner, paint "X" in center of each bell with charcoal. Using smallest end of stylus, place charcoal dot at ends of crossed lines.

5. Using #4 shader and kelly, paint reindeer's hat. Using #6 shader and deep clover, shade edge next to fur hatband and where hat folds over. (Some touch-up

work may be needed on hat after fur trim is painted.)

6. Using white and ⅛" deerfoot stippler, stipple fur trim on reindeer's hat. Do not cover sweatshirt fabric completely with paint; color of sweatshirt gives texture to the fur. When fur is stippled and dry, stipple charcoal onto areas where fur is overlapped by hat.

7. Using larger end of stylus and charcoal, paint oval eyes. Using liner and charcoal, add eyelashes and mouth. Using tip of liner brush handle and holly day red, paint nose. Using smaller end of stylus and white, dot highlights onto eyes.

8. Using #10 shader and gold fabric color, paint moon.

Heat-Setting & Finishing

1. When paints are completely dry, remove pins, remove shirt from painting board, and turn shirt inside out. Slip shirt over ironing board and heat-set paints by ironing wrong side of painted design for 20 seconds. Replace shirt on painting board; re-pin.

2. Thin crystal ice fabric color slightly with gel medium. Using #10 shader, apply thinned crystal ice to starry wave area.

3. Fit 20mm fine-line writer tip onto bottle of sparkling silver fabric color. *Before* crystal ice dries, write words using sparkling silver. Let dry.

4. Using #4 shader, apply a few highlights of crystal ice to snow. Add highlights to Santa's cheeks and right side of his head, unshaded sides of snow piles and snowballs, to right side of reindeer's head, to left side of muzzle, and to bottom body snowball on both Santa and reindeer. Let dry.

5. Brush white chalk marks from fabric with soft bristle brush. Remove pins; remove shirt from cardboard.

6. Let paint cure for at least five days before washing in cold water with mild soap. Line-dry.

What fun it is to color these bright holiday designs and then watch them shrink in the oven! Any young girl would love to wear one of these herself and make several others to give as Christmas friendship bracelets to her best school friends!

Instructions

1. Trace patterns onto shrinking plastic, tracing as many charms as desired. Cut out shapes with scissors.

2. Sand one side of each charm. Paint charms on sanded side. *Note: On samples, red stripes were painted on candy canes and peppermints; details were added to peppermint "wrappers" with black. Shanks of tree bulbs were painted with gold glitter; light bulbs and gumdrops were painted in assorted* colors; when dried, highlights were added with white. Let charms dry thoroughly.

3. Using hole punch, punch hole in each charm, taking care not to punch too close to edge.

4. Bake charms according to shrinking plastic package instructions.

5. Spray cooled charms with sealer; let dry.

6. Using needle-nose pliers, attach charms to bracelet with jump rings. ✿

Little Lady Bracelets

Designs by Deborah Brooks

Materials

- Aleene's Shrink-it O-Pake shrinking plastic
- Gold link bracelet
- Gold jump rings
- Fine sandpaper
- Acrylic paints: red, green, blue, yellow, purple, black, white and gold glitter
- Small paintbrushes
- Gloss-finish spray sealer
- Needle-nose pliers
- Hole punch

_A_dd a touch of class to a hairdo, a package or a bannister with this pretty dried flower arrangement on a velvet bow. The natural beauty of this ornament makes it one of long-lasting elegance.

Project Note
Refer to photo throughout for placement.

Instructions
1. "Gild" filbert, almond, hemlock cone and bruce cone by painting them with gold acrylic paint;

allow to dry completely.

2. Glue bow to barrette back.

3. Glue sprigs of boxwood onto bow to form background; add statice. Glue on cones and nuts as shown. Finish by gluing globe amaranths and Jackie berries.

Elegant Christmas Bow

Design by Creative Chi

Materials
- 6" burgundy velvet bow
- 2¾" barrette back
- Filbert in the shell
- Almond in the shell
- Botanicals from Creative Chi:
  Small hemlock cone
  Small bruce cone
  5 sprigs preserved boxwood
  8 sprigs white statice
  2 large birch cones
  2 small birch cones
  2 pink globe amaranths
  4 red Jackie berries
- True gold #DG37 Ultra Gloss Metallic acrylic paint from DecoArt
- Small paintbrush
- Crafty Magic Melt Super Flow Magic Pro low-temperature glue gun from Adhesive Technologies, Inc.

Wearing this happy little snowman on your snowsuit is a must for your next ski trip!

Project Note

Refer to photo throughout.

Instructions

1. Referring to pattern, cut two snowmen from flannel. Right sides facing, stitch snowman halves together about ⅛" from edge by machine or by hand, leaving an opening at top for turning. Turn snowman right side out, stuff and hand-stitch opening closed.

2. Using glue gun, attach ends of twigs at seams for arms.

3. Sew on black beads for eyes and red bead for nose. Glue buttons to front of body.

4. Using fine-point pen, add X's for mouth; with fingertip, apply cosmetic

blusher to make cheeks.

5. Fray edges of plaid or checked fabric strip; tie around neck for scarf.

6. For hat, sew shorter edges of T-shirt fabric together, right sides facing, to make tube. Run gathering stitch ½" from top of tube. Turn hat right side out; pull thread ends from gathering stitch to close top of hat; knot to secure. Fold up bottom edge of hat to make hatband. Glue hat to snowman's head.

7. Run silver cord over top of head and position pompoms at ends for earmuffs; glue in place.

8. Glue bow to hat. Glue pin back to back of snowman. ✏

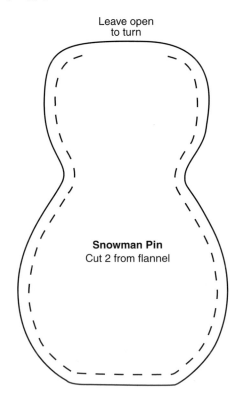

Leave open
to turn

Snowman Pin
Cut 2 from flannel

Snowman Pin

Design by Barbara A. Woolley

Materials

- 10" x 3" piece ivory, white or tea-dyed cotton flannel
- 5½" x 4½" piece knit T-shirt fabric
- 3½" x 1" strip tiny checked or plaid fabric
- ⅛" "E" beads: 2 black, 1 red
- 2 (½") buttons
- 2 (½") tan pompoms
- 2" piece silver cording
- ¾" bow tied from ⅛"-wide red satin ribbon
- 2 (1½") straight twigs
- Black waterproof fine-point marking pen
- Matching threads
- Hand-sewing needle
- Sewing machine (optional)
- Low-temperature glue gun
- Stuffing
- Pink cosmetic blusher
- 1" pin back

Stocking
Cut 2 from brown paper
reverse 1 for back

W ho would guess that the same
bag you used for carrying
home your Christmas packages
could be transformed into
these cute little pins? It's true!
Add paint, buttons, bows and a dash of
your own creativity—voilá!

Pattern Note

Refer to photo throughout.

Instructions

1. Referring to patterns, cut pin fronts and backs from brown paper. Base-coat right side of each piece with dark brown acrylic paint; let dry.

2. Apply crackle medium to all pieces; let dry as directed in manufacturer's instructions.

3. Paint pin fronts with acrylic paint: stocking cuff, toe and heel and mitten cuff with green; remainder of stocking and mitten with red. Paint back pieces red. Crackling should begin almost immediately. Let dry.

4. Using a paper towel, rub on a small amount of dark stain or glaze to enhance the pins' aged appearance. Let dry.

5. Apply varnish to fronts and backs of pins; let dry.

6. Using green and red glitter dimensional paints, add holly leaves and berries to pin fronts; let dry. Using black dimensional paint, add stitch lines as shown on pattern; let dry.

7. Using gold marking pen, write "Merry Christmas" on each pin; add veins to holly leaves with black pen. Let dry completely.

8. Glue on embellishments as desired: buttons, singly or in clusters; a small ribbon bow; "patches" of tiny fabric squares. Let dry.

9. Glue pin fronts to backs, wrong sides facing, by applying a bead of glue around the edges, inserting a bit of stuffing as you glue to give the pin dimension. Glue pin back to back of each pin. 🎁

Brown-Bag Pins

Designs by Barbara A. Woolley

Materials

- Brown paper bag
- Acrylic paints: dark brown, Christmas red, and green
- Dimensional paints in bottles with fine applicator tip: green, black and red glitter
- Crackle medium
- Dark stain or glaze
- Water-base varnish in satin or glossy finish
- Fine-point permanent marking pens: black and gold
- Embellishments:
  Tiny buttons
  2 tiny red ribbon bows
  Fabric scraps
- 2 small pin backs
- Polyester fiberfill
- Paintbrushes
- Tacky craft glue

Mitten
Cut 2 from brown paper
reverse 1 for back

Decorate It Christmas

ck the Halls With Crafts

Turn your home into a festival of enchanting Christmas decor! This collection of home decor items, from pretty wreaths to mini decorated trees, will add holiday charm to your home while letting you express your Christmas creativity!

H ere's a cheerful door decoration, brimming with gingerbread men, jingle bells and imitation candy canes!

1. Referring to patterns (page 63) and photo throughout, trace three gingerbread men onto tagboard. Using craft glue, glue tan felt to other side

of tagboard; cut out gingerbread shapes. Paint zigzag lines around edges using white slick dimensional paint; add eyes and smiles. Let dry. Dot black

Gingerbread & Snowflake Wreath

Design by Janna Britton

Materials

- 18" evergreen wreath
- Aerosol white flocking
- Slick dimensional fabric paints: black and white
- Scribbles glittering crystals dimensional paint from Duncan Enterprises
- 3 (7") pieces ¼"-wide red satin ribbon
- 3 (12") pieces ⅛"-wide red satin ribbon
- 6 (20") pieces 1½"-wide red velvet ribbon
- 3 yards 2"-wide red velvet ribbon with gold-wired edges
- 3 (12mm) red jingle bells
- 3 large red jingle bells
- 12 (8") plastic candy canes
- 12 (4") cinnamon sticks
- 9" x 12" sheet clear heavy-duty Mylar polyester film
- Craft glue
- Low-temperature glue gun
- 12" floral wire
- White tagboard
- 9" x 12" cashmere tan felt

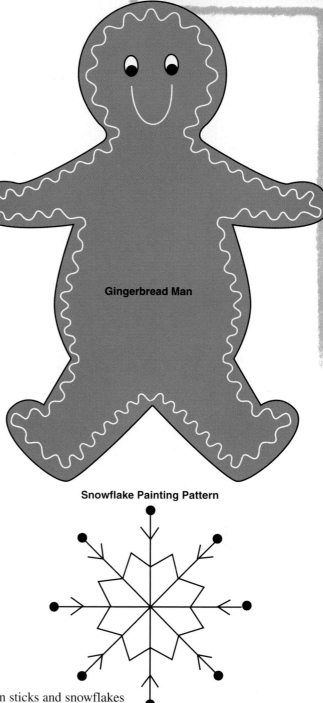

Gingerbread Man

Snowflake Painting Pattern

pupils onto eyes; let dry.

2. Tie each piece of ¼"-wide ribbon into a bow; glue one at each gingerbread man's neck. Glue small jingle bell to center of each bow.

3. Using glue gun, glue candy canes in crisscrossing pairs. Tie each piece of 1½"-wide velvet ribbon into bow; glue one to center of each candy cane pair.

4. Place polyester film over snowflake pattern. Using crystal paint, draw nine snowflakes. Let dry completely. Trim excess film from around painted snowflakes.

5. Working outside or in a well-ventilated area, spray flocking onto wreath. Affix a hanging loop made from floral wire to back of wreath.

6. Arrange gingerbread men, candy canes, cinnamon sticks and snowflakes around wreath.

7. Tie gold-edge velvet ribbon into a florist's bow with six 4" loops on each side. Leave 12" tails; notch ends of ribbon tails.

8. Wire bow to wreath; glue candy canes, cinnamon sticks, snowflakes and gingerbread men to wreath using glue gun.

9. Tie a large jingle bell to one end of each of the pieces of ⅛"-wide ribbon.

Hold all ribbons together; arrange so that center ribbon is shorter. Tie in a cluster to back of wreath so jingle bells appear to hang from large bow. ✍

Alternate white everlasting and ginger pieces up the spirals of a grapevine tree. Add nutmeg, celosia and star anise to the cones to create this back-to-nature ornamental tree.

Cinnamon Candle Tree

Design by Creative Chi

Materials

- Botanicals from Creative Chi:
  12"-tall twisted grapevine tree
  1 bunch preserved boxwood
  1 bunch red milo berries
  18–20 (1½"-long) thin cinnamon sticks
  20–25 sprigs white pearly everlasting
  15–20 pieces red celosia
  15–20 preserved dried ginger slices
  15–20 hemlock cones
  10–15 whole nutmegs
  12–14 star anise

- Crafty Magic Melt Super Flow Magic Pro low-temperature glue gun

Project Notes

Refer to photo throughout for placement.

To space the decorations evenly, you will need to make several half-spirals on the lower portion of the tree in addition to the full spirals.

Instructions

1. Glue boxwood sprigs and sprigs of red milo berries along the twisted spirals of grapevine.

2. Alternating white ever-lastings and ginger pieces, glue these pieces up spirals. Add whole nutmegs, celosia and star anise.

3. Glue thin cinnamon sticks upright from white everlastings to resemble candles; glue hemlock cones at or near base of candles to fill in design evenly.

4. Glue a cinnamon candle to top of tree; surround base of candle with box-wood and milo berries. 🖝

Beautify your dinner table with the natural elegance of nuts, dried berries and pinecones arranged in a painted plant holder. Make one or several to add candlelight charm to your home.

Christmas Candle Holder

Design by Creative Chi

Materials

- 3" clay flowerpot
- Americana acrylic paints from DecoArt:
  Snow white #DA1
  Alizarin crimson #DA179
  Santa red #DA170
- 8" taper candle
- Floral clay
- Copper-color candle cup
- Small piece red felt
- Botanicals from Creative Chi:
  Handful of oak moss
  2 almonds
  4 filberts
  2 acorns with caps
  4 hemlock cones
  3 red curly pods
  12–14 birch cones
  10–12 red jackie berries
  10 rose hips
  25–30 boxwood leaves
  5 sprigs white German statice
- Small piece of sponge
- Small paintbrush
- Low-temperature glue gun

Project Note

Refer to photo throughout for placement.

Instructions

1. Using paintbrush, base-coat flowerpot with alizarin crimson; when dry, sponge on accents with white and Santa red. Let dry.

2. Cut red felt to fit bottom of flowerpot; glue in place.

3. Fill flowerpot with floral clay, gluing candle cup in center.

4. Glue oak moss to top of pot to cover clay. Insert taper in candle cup. With candle in place, begin gluing nuts, acorns and hemlock cones to moss. Add red curly pods and birch cones. Fill in with jackie berries and rose hips, and finish with boxwood and statice sprigs. ✿

Project Note

Refer to photo throughout.

Instructions

1. Using sponge paintbrush, base-coat exterior of bottom half of box and sides of box top with rouge. Let dry.

2. Place lid on top of fabric; using pencil or chalk, trace outline of box, adding ½" all around. Cut out fabric shape; glue wrong side to top of box lid, centering fabric on lid.

3. Referring to pattern (page 68) and using transfer paper and pen, transfer outline of snowman, vest and hat to center of fabric on box lid. Do not transfer patterns for vest details or face at this time.

4. Using #8 flat brush, base-coat hat with black green, vest area with green sea, snowman with blue wisp and mittens with rouge.

5. Using #6 flat brush, highlight hat brim with green sea and then white: Wet brush, then dry on a paper towel; dip corner of brush into paint and stroke back and forth on paper until paint goes from dark color value to light color value; highlight design with color remaining in brush.

6. Dip scruffy brush into rouge and stipple mittens, making them look fuzzy. Highlight mittens by painting with scruffy brush dipped in white. Shade mittens by dipping scruffy brush in candy bar and stippling shaded areas.

7. Using scruffy brush, paint snowman by pouncing up and down with white. Do not clean brush. Dip one side of scruffy brush into blue wisp and shade snowman as directed on pattern.

8. Using clean paintbrush, add "snowdrifts" of white around base of snowman.

9. Trace face and vest details onto design. Using #1 liner brush and black paint, add eyelashes. Base-coat nose with black using #6 flat brush.

10. Dip a small piece of expandable sponge in water; squeeze out excess water. Dip into rouge paint and pounce up and down to paint cheeks.

11. Using #1 liner brush and black, paint mouth. Using white, dot highlights onto cheeks and nose.

12. Using #1 liner brush, paint lines on vest using red; dip point of brush in black green and add little dots at intersections of rouge lines. Let paint dry completely.

13. Referring to photo, glue buttons to design.

14. Cut ½" x ¾" piece of expandable sponge; dip into water and squeeze out excess. Dip sponge into white paint and stamp two rows of checkerboard pattern along bottom edge of box bottom. Let dry.

15. Apply varnish to exterior of box bottom and sides of box lid. Let dry.

16. Spatter snowman lightly with white paint: Dip old toothbrush into water, dry on paper towel, then dip into white paint. Draw wooden handle of #1 liner brush toward you across bristles to achieve spattering effect across snowman. (You may wish to practice technique on scrap paper first.) ✎

Top a tree-shaped box with a small calico print. Paint our snowman on your fabric and let him guard your Christmas treasure or help keep a surprise a secret.

Friendly Snowman Box

Design by Phyllis Sandford

Materials

- 12" Christmas-tree–shape papier-mâché box
- 14" square small-print calico
- 4 assorted red and green flat buttons
- Ceramcoat acrylic paints from Delta Technical Coatings, Inc.:
  Black green #02-116
  Rouge #02-404
  Candy bar #02-407
  Green sea #02-445
  Blue wisp #02-455
  White #02-505
  Black #02-506
- Glossy exterior varnish
- White craft glue
- Daler Rowney/Robert Simmons Tole Master paintbrushes:
  #6 and #8 flat shaders #T60
  #1 liner #T51
- Old, scruffy paintbrush
- Old toothbrush
- 1" sponge paintbrush
- Expandable sponge
- Pencil or tailor's chalk
- Transfer paper
- Pen

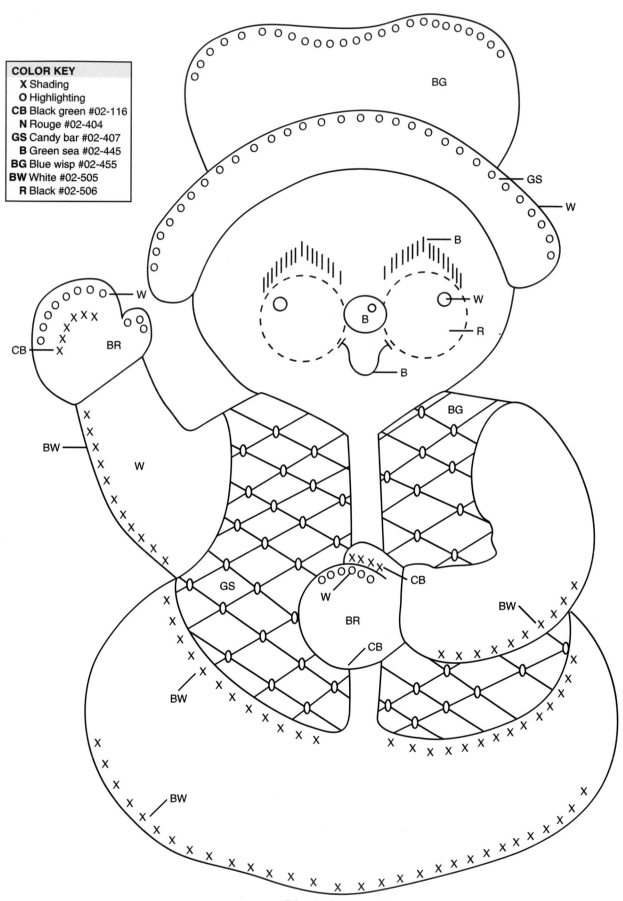

COLOR KEY
X Shading
O Highlighting
CB Black green #02-116
N Rouge #02-404
GS Candy bar #02-407
B Green sea #02-445
BG Blue wisp #02-455
BW White #02-505
R Black #02-506

Friendly Snowman Box

Play hide-and-seek with shy little Rudolph as he hides among your plants. His big red felt nose is sure to help you identify this favorite Christmas character!

Reindeer Plant Poke

Design by Debi Schmitz

Materials

- Rainbow Classic Felt from Kunin Felt:
  1 sheet cashmere tan
  4" square kelly green
  3" square red
- 9" slender wooden dowel or skewer
- Tan acrylic craft paint
- Paintbrush
- 1¼" wooden circle from Forster Inc.
- ½" silver jingle bell
- Black #5 pearl cotton
- #20 needle
- Polyester fiberfill
- 2 (18mm) movable round or oval eyes
- 18" x ½" strip torn from Christmas-print fabric
- Craft glue

Eyelid

Holly

Project Note

Refer to photo throughout for placement.

Instructions

1. Trace outline of a child's hand on paper, tracing four fingers only. Cut out. Using paper pattern, cut two matching shapes from cashmere tan felt.

2. Using pearl cotton, blanket-stitch felt pieces together, leaving a 2" opening at bottom for stuffing. Stuff lightly and stitch opening shut.

3. Paint dowel with tan paint and let dry. Apply glue to blunt end; carefully insert up through bottom of stuffed shape.

4. Cut 1¼" circle from red felt; glue to wooden circle for nose. Glue nose to reindeer's head.

5. Cut two eyelids from cashmere tan felt. Glue movable eyes to face; glue eyelids overlapping eyes.

6. Cut three holly leaves from kelly green felt; glue in cluster at top of head.

7. Tear fabric strip in half. Tie one half in bow and glue atop holly leaves; glue jingle bell to holly and bow. Tie remaining fabric in bow around dowel at base of head.

L et these refrigerator friends keep you and your family posted as they hold your notes, pictures and to-do lists with the magnets in their hands and feet. Their whimsical expressions and various poses will delight you!

Basic Construction

1. Referring to patterns (pages 71 and 72), cut two bodies per friend from felt.

2. Using 6 strands matching

Fridgie Friends

Designs by Bev George

Materials

Each Friend

- 5 (¾") round magnets
- Fabric paints: black, red glitter and pearly white
- Small paintbrush
- Sewing needle
- Black fine-point permanent marking pen
- Polyester fiberfill
- Pencil with eraser
- Steam iron
- Craft glue

Each Gingerbread Friend

- 9" x 12" piece cashmere tan or putty brown Rainbow Classic Felt from Kunin Felt
- 6-strand embroidery floss to match felt
- Small red ribbon bow
- Scrap of red print fabric
- Small piece of iron-on adhesive
- Iridescent glitter glue

Each Teddy Bear Friend

- 9" x 12" piece copper or cinnamon Rainbow Classic Felt from Kunin Felt
- 6-strand embroidery floss to match felt
- Narrow red ribbon
- Scrap of red print fabric
- Small piece of iron-on adhesive
- 5mm black pompom
- Gold glitter glue

Each Snowman Friend

- Rainbow Classic Felt from Kunin Felt:
  9" x 12" piece white
  Small pieces of black
- White 6-strand embroidery floss
- Narrow red ribbon or ⅜"-wide red-and-green braid
- Small red fabric bow (optional)
- Orange fabric paint

Teddy Bear Ear
Cut 4 for each

Large Heart

Teddy Bear Muzzle
Cut 1 for each

Small Heart

floss, blanket-stitch around body from neck to neck. As you stitch, insert a magnet in each hand and foot, securing in place with a small tack stitch. *Note: The positive and negative sides of each magnet will dictate what each hand, foot and belly will hold. Using varied combinations will add personality to your friends.*

3. Drop fifth magnet in friend's tummy; enclose with a running stitch across neck opening.

4. Blanket-stitch three-quarters of the way around head; stuff head and close opening with blanket stitch.

5. Refer to patterns and facial diagrams (page 72) and finishing instructions that follow to complete each friend, dipping eraser end of pencil in black paint to dot-stamp eyes.

Gingerbread Friends

1. Use permanent marker to draw eyelashes, cheek lines, nose and mouth. Add dot of red glitter paint to tongue and dots of pearly white paint to eyes for highlights.

2. For girl, iron adhesive to back of red fabric; cut out apron and iron onto gingerbread, bending straps to back. Outline apron and add hair with pearly white paint; let dry. Glue bow to hair.

3. For boy, iron adhesive to back of red fabric; cut out one large and six small heart appliqués and iron in a "string" across gingerbread. Link hearts and add hair with pearly white paint; outline hearts and add highlights to hair with iridescent glitter

glue; let dry. Glue red ribbon bow to neck.

Teddy Bear Friends

1. Cut one muzzle and four ears for each teddy bear from felt scraps; glue ears together in pairs.

2. Use permanent marker to draw eyelashes on head; draw mouth on muzzle and detail lines on ears. Add dot of red glitter paint to tongue and dots of pearly white paint for eye highlights.

3. Glue ears and muzzle to head; glue black pompom to top of muzzle for nose.

4. Iron adhesive onto back of red fabric; cut out one large heart appliqué and glue to body; outline with gold glitter glue. Tie red ribbon bow around neck. Or, using red glitter paint, paint hearts down front of bear; glue red ribbon bow at neckline.

Snowman Friends

1. Cut one hat brim and one 2" x 1½" hat crown from black felt. Fold hat crown in half so it measures 1" x 1½" and secure with glue. Slip raw edges through slit in brim; glue hat to snowman's head.

2. Use permanent marker to draw on eyelashes. Using black paint, dot on mouth. Using pearly white paint, dot on eye highlights. Using orange paint, paint nose.

3. Tie red ribbon hatband around hat crown. Using black paint, add buttons down front of snowman; glue red fabric bow at neckline. Or, tie hatband and matching neck scarf of red-and-green braid; paint heart buttons down front of snowman using red glitter paint. ✂

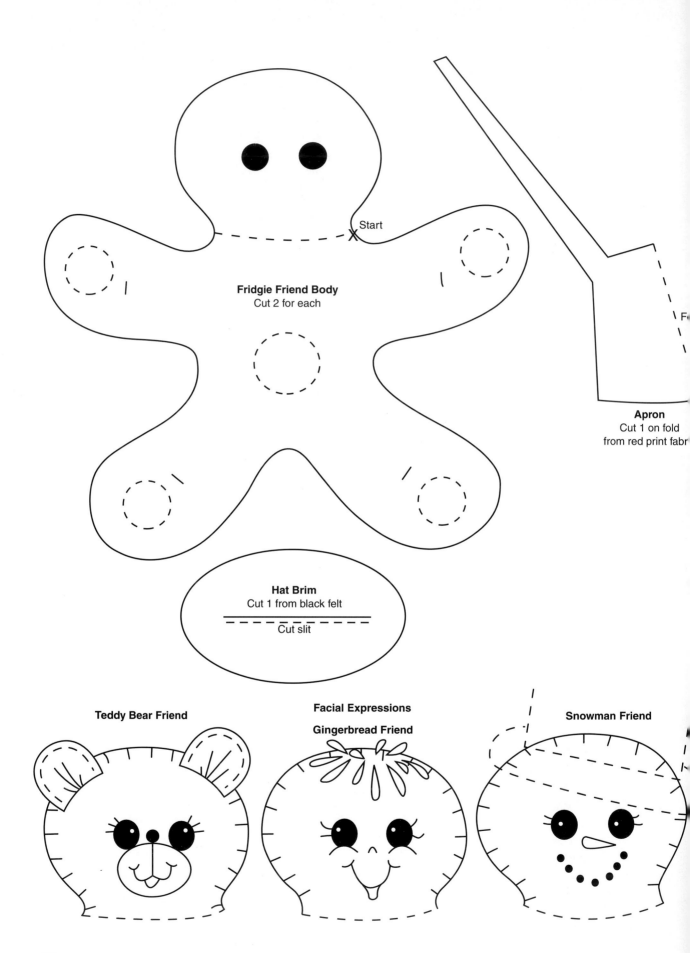

Fridgie Friend Body
Cut 2 for each

Start

Apron
Cut 1 on fold
from red print fabr

Hat Brim
Cut 1 from black felt

Cut slit

Teddy Bear Friend

Facial Expressions

Gingerbread Friend

Snowman Friend

There is a legend that says that a bird in your tree will bring you and yours good luck, may this bring you happiness

Bring the beauty of winter birds inside your home with these brightly painted cutouts. Add dowel rods or clothespins and put them in so many places.

Cardinal Creations

Designs by Delores Ruzicka

Materials

Cardinals

- Scraps of ¾"-thick pine
- Ceramcoat acrylic paints from Delta Technical Coatings, Inc.:
  Bright red #02-503
  White #02-505
  Black #02-506
  Barn red #02-490
- American Painter paintbrushes from Loew-Cornell:
  #3/0 liner #2369
  #3 brush #2372
  #8 flat brush #4300
- Scroll saw or band saw
- Fine-grit sandpaper
- Satin-finish varnish

Ornaments

- 4" twigs of artificial evergreen or small amounts of dried Spanish moss
- Small sprigs of dried German statice
- Wooden clip clothespins
- Walnut gel stain
- Small pieces of card stock
- Hot-glue gun with wood glue sticks

Plant or Wreath Pokes

- ¼"-diameter dowel
- Walnut gel stain
- Drill with ¼" bit
- Hot-glue gun with wood glue sticks

Cardinals

1. Referring to pattern, trace onto pine (see General Instructions, page 175). Cut out with scroll saw or band saw; sand until smooth.

2. Using #8 flat brush, paint each cardinal bright red, using two coats if necessary. When dry, use #3 brush to paint beak and area around eye with black. Using black, add detail to wings, crown and tail with #3/0 liner. Let dry.

3. Using #3/0 liner and white paint, paint small oval at eye. When dry, paint small black circle inside white oval. Add tiny white dot to black circle for eye highlight.

4. Using #3 brush and barn red, shade wing, tail and breast. Let dry.

5. Coat with varnish.

Ornament

1. Stain wooden clothespin with walnut gel stain; let dry.

2. Glue base of bird to flat surface of clothespin. Glue two 2" twigs of artificial pine or sprigs of Spanish moss to base of bird to hide clothespin. Add a small sprig of German statice.

3. Write this verse on card stock and attach to each bird: "There is a legend that says that a bird in a tree means good luck. May this bird bring you and yours good luck and much happiness."

Plant or Wreath Poke

1. Apply walnut gel stain to dowel; let dry. Cut dowel desired length.

2. Drill ¼" hole in base of bird; glue end of dowel in hole.

*T*he simple beauty of this cross is sure to add serenity to your Christmas reflections. Lovely poinsettias painted on this dimensional wooden cross will bring peace to your holiday season.

Poinsettia Cross

Design by Sandra McCooey

Materials

- 6" x 10" piece 1"-thick wood
- Sandpaper
- Transfer paper
- Stylus
- FolkArt acrylic paints from Plaid Enterprises, Inc.:
  Sunflower #432
  Pure gold #660
  Rose chiffon #753
  Tapioca #903
  Robin's egg #915
  Raspberry sherbet #966
- Paintbrushes:
  #2 liner
  #4 round
  ½" flat
- Palette or plastic foam plate
- ⅔ yard 1"-wide metallic gold wire-edge ribbon
- Band saw or saber saw
- Router with small bit (optional)
- Aerosol matte- or glossy-finish varnish
- Small eye screw

Poinsettia Cross

Dampen flower petals on cross with moist brush, then pick up some of the thinned paint and touch petals with tip of brush to add color. Color will spread into dampened spots.

4. Referring to steps 2 and 3, make paint wash with raspberry paint. Use to highlight parts of petals. Paint will flow only into dampened areas, so leave some spots dry so they will remain lighter.

5. Referring to steps 2 and 3, make paint wash with robin's egg; paint leaves.

6. Use robin's egg wash to paint pine branches. Add a second coat, if desired, for darker color.

7. Load #4 round brush with raspberry wash and follow ribbon line, using varying pressure as you move from poinsettia to pine branch to vary ribbon's width.

8. Dot berries onto pine branches by dipping end of wooden paintbrush handle into undiluted paints and touching lightly to design, making some berries raspberry and some rose.

9. Referring to step 8, add dots to center of poinsettia with undiluted sunflower.

Finishing

1. Spray painted cross with matte or glossy varnish; let dry thoroughly.

2. Screw small eye screw into top of cross.

3. Fold ribbon in half lengthwise; push through eye screw from back to front. Tie ribbon in bow with knot around screw. ✎

Project Notes

Refer to photo throughout.

Let paint dry thoroughly between applications of different colors.

Preparation & Base Coats

1. Referring to pattern (page 74), transfer cross outline to wood (see General Instructions, page 175). Cut out, using saw. Add decorative edge around top, if desired, using router bit. Sand until smooth.

2. Base-coat top surface with tapioca. Base-coat sides with robin's egg. Base-coat routed edges with pure gold.

3. When all paint is thoroughly dry, sand lightly to remove any roughness. Base-coat surfaces again.

Painting Design

1. Transfer pattern to painted top of cross using very light pressure (lines may show beneath paint).

2. Pour pea-size drop of rose chiffon onto palette. Dip brush into clear water, dropping some onto palette next to paint. Touch tip of brush into paint and pull into water puddle, stirring to thin paint. This creates a wash that closely resembles watercolor.

3. Rinse brush; blot thoroughly on paper towel.

ool the eye with these fun "special effects" and enjoy displaying the resulting bell-pull-style decoration.

String of Ornaments

Design by Kathy Wegner

Materials

- 9" x 12" piece ½"-thick wood
- Drill with 5/32" bit
- Scroll saw
- Wood sealer
- FolkArt acrylic paints from Plaid Enterprises, Inc.:
  Pure gold #660
  Berries 'n cream #752
  Robin's egg #915
- Decorator Glazes from Plaid Enterprises, Inc.:
  Burgundy #53017
  Malachite green #53046
- Multipurpose comb #30124 from Plaid Enterprises, Inc.
- Sea sponge
- 12" jute twine
- Wood glue
- Matte varnish

Project Note

Work with one piece at a time when glazing and decorating painted pieces. If results are not pleasing, wipe off paint with damp sponge and try again. Refer to photo throughout. Leave backs of pieces plain, or decorate as you wish.

Instructions

1. Referring to patterns (page 77), cut one of each shape from wood; drill ¼"-deep holes into top and/or bottom edges of each piece as indicated.

2. Base-coat sides and edges of wooden pieces: Use robin's egg on stocking and tree, using pure gold on tree trunk; use berries 'n cream on heart and ornament, using pure gold on ornament cap. Let dry; apply second coat.

3. Glaze robin's egg portion of tree with malachite green in scallop pattern using malachite edge of comb.

4. Glaze stocking with malachite green in vertical stripes using marquetry edge of comb.

5. Glaze heart with burgundy in a blotchy pattern using sea sponge.

6. Glaze berries 'n cream portion of ornament with burgundy in crisscross diagonal lines using bird's-eye edge of comb.

7. Allow all pieces to dry overnight. Coat with matte varnish; let dry.

8. Put wood glue in drilled holes; press in ends of short pieces of jute twine to join pieces. Push a hanging loop of jute into hole in top of tree. Let glue dry thoroughly. ❦

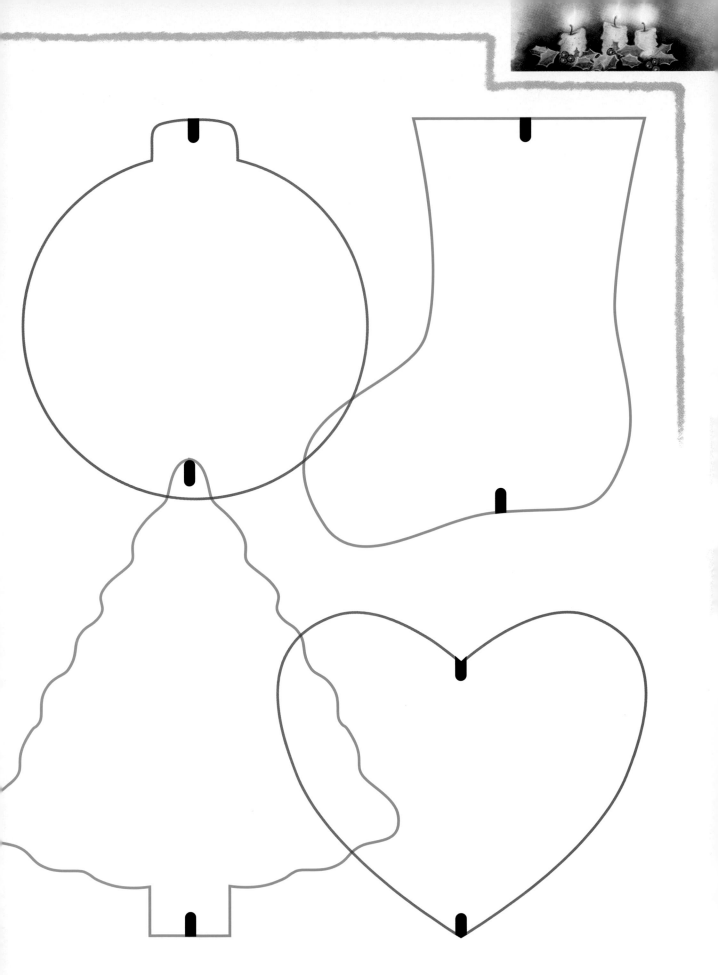

Serve It Christmas
Crafts for the Hostess

Whether you're looking for charming accents to make your holiday guests feel at home, or looking for quick-to-craft hostess gifts, this chapter brings you a festive collection of decorations, gifts, table sets and more that will make this year's holiday hospitality extra-special.

Turn a large coffee can into this festive table decoration with a little paint, a bouquet of artificial holly and a cheery plaid bow!

Holly Centerpiece

Design by Paula Bales

Materials

- 7"-tall x 6"-diameter coffee can
- Off-white aerosol metal primer
- Americana acrylic paints from DecoArt:
  Sand #DA4
  Evergreen #DA82
  Santa red #DA170
- ½"-thick household sponge
- Small piece of heavy paper
- Short section of ⅜"-diameter wooden dowel
- Black fine-point permanent marking pen
- 2½"-wide holiday plaid ribbon
- Floral foam
- Silk holly branches

Holly Leaf

Project Note

Refer to photo throughout for placement.

Instructions

1. Spray can inside and out with two coats of metal primer, letting primer dry between coats.

2. Using a small piece of the household sponge, dab a coat of sand paint over surface of the can. Let dry.

3. From heavy paper cut a stencil of holly leaf pattern (above). Rinse a small piece of sponge in water; squeeze out excess and dip sponge in evergreen paint. Blot off excess. Stamp holly leaves around bottom of can, using stencil.

4. Dip end of dowel in Santa red paint; stamp holly berries on can. Let paints dry.

5. Outline leaves and berries and draw tendrils with black permanent marking pen.

6. Tie ribbon around top of can in a multiloop bow.

7. Place floral foam in can; arrange silk holly branches as desired.

Fill this lovely basket with pine- or cinnamon-scented potpourri and tuck it on a shelf to delight guests with its lovely appearance and relaxing aroma.

Enlarge holly border 130% to return it to its original size.

Potpourri Basket

Design by Creative Chi

Materials

- 9½" x 5½" basket with 2½"–2¾" straight sides
- Botanicals from Creative Chi:
  110–120 (2½") cinnamon sticks
  3 dried apple slices
  4 dried orange-peel ribbons
  2 whole almonds
  2 whole filberts
  2 whole nutmegs
  3 star anise
  6 birch cones
  2 pieces dried ginger
  15 dried cranberries
  4 (½") cinnamon sticks
  5 sprigs preserved boxwood
- 1 sheet Fun Foam craft foam by Westrim Crafts
- Low-temperature glue gun

Project Note

Refer to photo throughout for placement.

Instructions

1. Glue larger cinnamon sticks around outside of basket; glue additional cinnamon sticks along top edge of basket, if desired.

2. In one corner, glue apple slices. Then glue orange-peel ribbons to form a bow shape. Arrange nuts and nutmegs, and finish with star anise, birch cones, ginger, cranberries, small cinnamon sticks and boxwood.

3. Cut craft foam to fit bottom of basket; glue in place.

Touch of Gold Table Set

Designs by Susan Schultz

Make your Christmas dinner a star-studded affair with this very easy-to-craft set including a place mat, napkin, napkin ring, centerpiece, place card and candle holder.

Materials

- Tall wooden star #12800 from Walnut Hollow
- Materials from West Coast Wood Craft Supply:
  8 (1") primitive stars
  2 (1½") primitive stars
  2 (2") primitive stars
  2 (1¾") moons
  3" pointed star
  1½" candle cup
  1¾" grooved napkin ring
- Ceramcoat Crackle medium from Delta Technical Coatings, Inc.
- Clear Ceramcoat Faux Finish Glaze Base from Delta Technical Coatings, Inc.
- Light ivory #02-401 Ceramcoat acrylic paint from Delta Technical Coatings, Inc.
- 14K gold #02-604 Ceramcoat Gleams paint from Delta Technical Coatings, Inc.
- Satin-finish water-base varnish from Delta Technical Coatings, Inc.
- Starry tree #95-527-0012 Stencil Magic pre-cut stencil from Delta Technical Coatings, Inc.
- Tole Master paintbrushes from Robert Simmons Brushes:
  #1 liner
  #6 flat
  ¾" flat
  ¼" stencil brush
  #6 flat fabric brush
- Natural oval place mat from BagWorks
- Natural dinner napkin from BagWorks
- Wood glue
- ScotchGard fabric protector from 3M
- 10"–12" gold taper candle
- Fine-grit sandpaper
- Tack cloth
- Small natural sponge

Project Notes

Refer to photo throughout.

Allow paint and other finishes to dry thoroughly between coats unless instructed otherwise.

Instructions

Preparation

1. Lightly sand all wooden pieces; wipe off dust with tack cloth. Apply a light coat of satin-finish varnish to seal; let dry thoroughly. Lightly sand and wipe again with tack cloth.

2. Apply two coats of gold paint to moons and all stars, front and back, except one 2" star; apply gold paint also to outer edges and inside of napkin ring.

3. Apply two coats of light ivory paint to unpainted 2" star and to candle cup and middle of napkin ring.

Centerpiece

1. Using ¾" brush, apply a generous, even coat of crackle medium to one side of each star centerpiece. Set timer for 20 minutes. *Note: Crackle medium should not dry; it is ready while it still looks slightly glossy. In a very dry area, the crackle medium will dry more quickly, so pay attention to the time and check it often.*

2. Mix one part light ivory paint to one part faux finish glaze base. Generously load

¾" brush with mixture and apply to each surface that has been brushed with crackle medium. Start on the left and move quickly across to the right, always picking up more paint. Do not over-stroke, dig brush into the wood or go back over a painted area with brush, or paint will lift off. Work quickly and evenly; cracks will follow brush strokes.

3. Repeat steps 1 and 2 on remaining surfaces and edges of centerpiece. Allow each side to dry thoroughly.

4. Assemble star centerpiece. Glue seven 1" gold stars and both gold moons to sides; glue 1½" gold star to very top of centerpiece.

Napkin & Place Mat

1. Using fabric brush, paint edges of place mat with gold paint.

2. Randomly stencil stars on napkin and place mat by loading stencil brush lightly with gold paint and tapping into star opening on stencil. Do not load brush too heavily; blot excess paint off onto paper towel before applying brush to fabric surface. Let dry.

3. Apply fabric protector to place mat following manufacturer's directions.

Napkin Ring

1. Referring to step 2 for Napkin & Place Mat, sten-

cil stars on light ivory portion of napkin ring.

2. Glue 1½" gold star to center of napkin ring.

Candle Holder

1. Wet sponge; squeeze out excess water. Pick up a little

gold paint and apply to top rim of candle cup. Stencil some gold stars on candle cup, referring to step 2 of Napkin & Place Mat.

2. Glue a gold 1" star to side of candle cup; glue base of

candle cup to center of gold 3" star.

3. Insert candle into cup.

Place Card

1. Wet sponge; squeeze out all excess water. Pick up a little gold paint and apply

to edges of one 2" light ivory star.

2. Glue light ivory star to front of 2" gold star. Using liner brush and gold paint, add name to front of light ivory star.

Shrinky Dinks Napkin Rings

Designs by Betty Morris

Materials
Both Projects

- *2 Shrinky Dinks Bright White Shrinkable Creative Packs*
- *Speedball Fineline Painter paint markers: red, green, yellow, pink and black*
- *Black fine-line permanent marking pen*
- *Large spool*
- *Tape*

1. Read instructions on Shrinky Dinks packs before beginning; follow manufacturer's directions.

2. Tape shrinkable plastic to Love Doves or Santa pattern (pages 85 and 86). Trace design with black permanent marking pen.

3. Color in design, referring to patterns.

4. Personalize with your name and date using black permanent marking pen, if desired; cut out.

5. Following instructions on package, bake napkin rings. Remove from oven.

6. When cool enough to handle, color edges with paint markers. Return napkin rings to oven colored side down and bake until resoftened, 3–5 minutes.

7. Remove from oven and quickly roll softened plastic around spool of thread, beginning at one end of plastic. Let cool and remove from spool.

8. If shape is not satisfactory, try returning the piece to the oven for 3–5 minutes and softening it to reshape it. Cooled napkin rings are washable. ❦

Shrinky Dink Love Doves

Shrinky Dink Santa

ive your party guests a special favor decorated with dried flowers, berries and pinecones. It's so pretty, they won't want to open it!

Project Note

Refer to photo throughout. For specific materials used for each ornament, refer to instructions for Individual Favors that follow.

General Assembly

1. Wrap cardboard tube in gift wrap, securing with glue and folding paper ends into tube. Wrap trinkets and candy in tissue paper and slide into tube.

2. Wrap tube with gold net; tie ends with bows of picot-edge ribbon. Wrap plaid ribbon around each tube over gold net; glue in place.

3. Paint nuts and cones gold as desired; let dry. Add decoration to cracker by gluing on foliage sprigs first, then adding nuts and cones. Fill in with small flowers and berries as shown in photo.

Individual Favors

Red Favor: Use red-and-gold gift wrap, gold tissue paper, red picot-edge ribbon, five boxwood sprigs, two gilded birch cones, one gilded filbert, three gilded hemlock cones and three strawberry globe amaranths.

White Favor: Use white gift wrap, white tissue paper, white picot-edge ribbon, two boxwood sprigs, two cedar sprigs, two gilded birch cones, two gilded filberts, three sprigs of white statice and three jackie berries.

Green Favor: Use green gift wrap, green tissue paper, green picot-edge ribbon, seven cedar sprigs, one gilded filbert, two gilded hemlock cones, two sprigs of white statice and three jackie berries.

Cracker Favors

Designs by Creative Chi

Materials
Each Cracker

- 4" section cut from a cardboard paper towel or bathroom tissue roll
- 1 or 2 trinkets and a hard candy
- ¼ sheet colored tissue paper
- 6" square gift wrap
- 8" 1¼"-wide red plaid ribbon
- 6" x 12" piece gold mesh fabric or wide ribbon
- 2 (8") pieces coordinating picot-edge satin ribbon
- Assorted botanicals from Creative Chi (see instructions for Individual Favors)
- True gold #DG37 Ultra Gloss Metallic acrylic paint from DecoArt
- Small paintbrush
- Low-temperature glue gun

Adorn a small heart-shaped wreath with pretty Christmas decorations such as golden holly leaves, berries and an angel figure to add an elegant touch to your holiday decor.

Holly & Berries Wreath

Design by Vivian Holland-Medina

Materials

- 6" Spanish moss heart wreath
- 16" length of mini-berry garland
- Metallic gold spray paint (optional)
- 7 clusters of small metallic gold holly leaves
- Miniature angel or cherub ornament
- 8" gold net ribbon
- 2 floral picks of small round metallic gold berries with green silk leaves
- Hot-glue gun

Project Note

Refer to photo throughout for placement.

Instructions

1. Cut garland of mini-berries in half; spray some of the garland with gold paint, if desired; let dry.

2. Bend garland halves to fit shape of heart wreath. Apply garland to wreath with small amounts of hot glue where berries touch wreath; do not over-glue.

3. Fold under stem ends of gold berries clusters. Glue one cluster on each side of the heart, on top of the mini-berry garland. Shape green silk leaves; apply a bit of glue if necessary.

4. Apply clusters of small gold holly leaves: two at lower point of heart, two under tip of heart, two above gold berry clusters and one at center top of wreath.

5. Cut gold net ribbon in half; fold and tie each half in a knot. Glue one at lower center, under holly leaves, and one above gold berries on left side.

6. Glue angel ornament directly above gold berries on left side.

D ecorated with clusters of nuts, cinnamon sticks, seed pods, pinecones and dried berries, this handsome tree will appeal to nature lovers of all ages.

Nature's Bounty Christmas Tree

Design by Creative Chi

Materials

- 18″ twisted grapevine Christmas tree
- Botanicals from Creative Chi:
  1 bunch preserved boxwood
  24–30 (3″) cinnamon sticks
  15–20 whole nutmegs
  18–24 hemlock cones
  48 rose hips
  24–30 preserved dried ginger slices
  20–30 whole allspice berries
  10–12 star anise
  10–12 birch cones
- Low-temperature glue gun

Project Note

Refer to photo throughout.

Instructions

1. Glue boxwood sprigs and cinnamon sticks along the line of the tree's ribs, spacing evenly.

2. Decorate alternating cinnamon-boxwood bunches with a whole nutmeg, a hemlock cone, two rose hips, a ginger slice and an allspice berry.

3. Decorate remaining cinnamon-boxwood bunches with a star anise, a ginger slice, two rose hips and a birch cone.

4. Decorate very top of tree with a nutmeg; surround base of this treetop arrangement with boxwood sprigs.

CHEERS

Tamela

Jen

Arlou

Quick-as-a-Wink Place Cards
Instructions begin on page 92

Here's a quick hostess gift idea. Use an easy glass-etching technique to etch a carafe, pick out a pretty plaid ribbon and fill the carafe with your hostess's favorite wine. She'll love it!

Holiday Carafe

Design by Maggie Rampy

Materials

- Wooden toothpick
- 1" masking tape
- ½-liter glass wine carafe
- 4½" x 5" piece self-adhesive vinyl
- ¼" vinyl stick-on letters
- 2 pairs ⅝" adhesive-back Velcro hook-and-loop fastener rounds (optional)
- 4-ounce jar Etchall etching creme from B&B Products
- Etchall squeegee from B&B Products
- 24" piece ribbon
- 2 clean dish towels

Project Notes

Refer to photo throughout.

1. Transfer tree pattern onto center of self-adhesive vinyl. Mark center at top and bottom of tree; fold self-adhesive vinyl in half at center marking and cut out tree, leaving solid border of self-adhesive vinyl around cutout.

2. Place 5" strip of masking tape 2" from bottom of carafe; stick-on letters will be aligned along top of masking tape. Attach top of each letter to the point of a toothpick; press letter down. When all letters are in place, remove masking tape.

3. Remove backing from self-adhesive vinyl; place tree opening on carafe, centering bottom of tree below stick-on letters. Some darts may develop in self-adhesive vinyl as you smooth it onto carafe; press them as smooth as possible with your finger.

4. Lay a frame or ring of masking tape around the tree opening on the self-adhesive vinyl border to keep etching creme in area to be etched. When tape is in place, it will look like a small bowl around the tree opening.

5. With clean towel, remove all fingerprints from area to be etched. Lay carafe flat on a dish towel; roll a second dish towel and place under neck of carafe to keep it flat and stable.

6. Pour a generous amount of etching creme in the area at the top of the tree. Using squeegee, lightly pull creme over entire tree opening all at one time. Make sure design is completely covered and creme goes onto self-adhesive vinyl border, beyond cut lines. Let stand undisturbed for 15 minutes.

7. Pinch corner of masking tape to make a trough and scrape creme back into jar, using squeegee. Save as much of the creme as possible as it can be used over and over.

8. Rinse carafe thoroughly under running water, taking care not to let creme run onto unetched glass as it is rinsed off; this could streak the exposed glass. Dry carafe with a soft clean towel.

9. Tie ribbon in bow around neck. Or, make a removable bow: Cut an 8" piece of ribbon and attach fastener rounds to each end of ribbon so ribbon can be fastened around neck of bottle. Make a 3½" bow from remaining ribbon; put half of one fastener round pair on back of bow and the other half on ribbon on bottle. Trim tails on ribbon bow as desired.

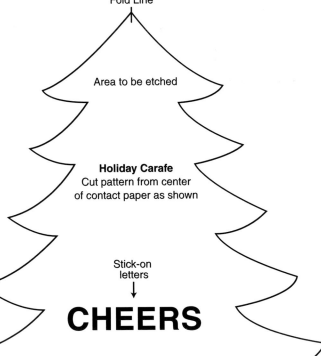

Fold Line

Area to be etched

Holiday Carafe
Cut pattern from center
of contact paper as shown

Stick-on
letters
↓

CHEERS

Fold Line

Youngsters will love joining in on the fun of making these super-easy foam place cards including a Christmas tree and star.

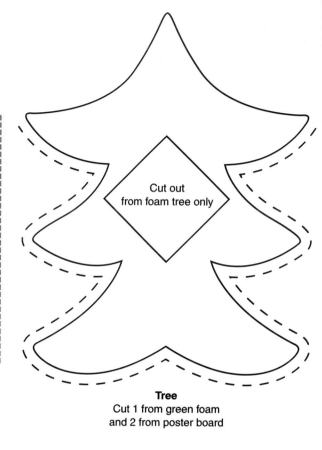

Quick-as-a-Wink Place Cards

Designs by Crystal Ogle • Shown on page 90

Materials
- Poster board or colored file folders
- Craft foam: green and white
- Craft glue
- Sharp pointed object such as embossing tool or dry ink pen

Cut out from foam tree only

Tree
Cut 1 from green foam and 2 from poster board

Christmas Tree

1. Referring to patterns cut two trees from poster board and one from green craft foam.

2. Lay foam tree atop one of the poster-board trees. Apply a bit of glue around edges only, leaving the top unglued so paper with name on it can be slid into holder (refer to dotted line on pattern for glue placement).

3. Using a ruler or other straight edge and beginning at the top, score remaining poster-board tree down center with embossing tool; fold in half along scored line. Glue half of scored tree to back of place card; fold out unglued half to make easel.

4. When glue is completely dry, slide in a piece of paper on which name is typed or written.

Star

Follow steps 1–4 for tree, substituting white foam for green and star pattern for tree pattern.

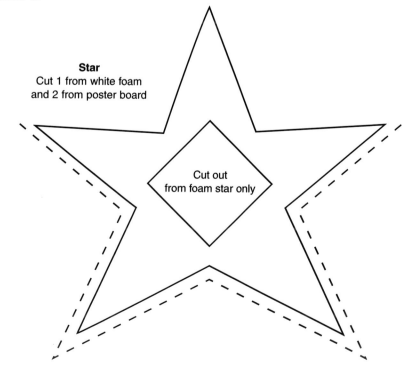

Star
Cut 1 from white foam and 2 from poster board

Cut out from foam star only

Add a charming country touch to your holiday table with this set of place mats and napkins. Fusible web and fabric paints make this project a snap for crafters of all skill levels.

Country Snowmen Table Set

Designs by Barbara A. Woolley • Shown on page 94

Materials
2 Napkins & Place Mats

- 2 ready-made red-and-black checked place mats
- 2 red fabric napkins
- 2 natural-wood napkin rings
- ⅓ yard HeatnBond iron-on adhesive from Therm O Web
- 4 (6mm) white pompoms
- Scribbles dimensional fabric paint writers by Duncan Enterprises: black, orange and glittery silver
- ⅓ yard each of 3 different coordinating green print or checked fabrics for trees
- 12" square Warm & Natural batting from Warm Products, Inc.
- 10" square fabric for jackets
- 10" square yellow fabric for stars
- 6" square fabric for hats
- 6" square fabric for scarves
- 6" square fabric for mittens
- Steam iron
- Fabric glue
- Tacky craft glue
- Cosmetic blusher
- Cotton swab

Mitten
Cut 2, reverse 1,
for each snowman

Project Notes
Refer to photo throughout.

The following fabric choices were used on sample projects: assorted forest-and-tan checks for trees; coordinating navy-and-tan check for jackets; white-pin-dot-on-navy fabric for hats; gold-printed forest green for scarves; and tan print for mittens.

Place Mats
1. Launder place mats in warm water using mild soap; do not use fabric softener.

2. Fuse iron-on adhesive onto wrong sides of batting and fabrics. Referring to patterns (below and page 95), cut snowmen from batting and other pieces from fabrics.

3. Using photo as a guide and following iron-on adhesive manufacturer's instructions, fuse pieces in place: a small, medium and large tree on the left side; a large tree on the right, followed by snowman, hat, jacket, scarf, mittens and star.

4. Using black paint writer throughout, outline each pattern piece, making an occasional large X-stitch as you go. Add fringe to ends of scarf.

5. Using silvery paint writer, add stars to place mat as desired.

6. Using fabric glue, glue a pompom to tip of each hat.

7. Using cotton swab, dot a little cosmetic blusher onto snowman's cheeks. Draw nose onto snowman with orange paint writer. Using black paint writer, dot on eyes and smaller dots for mouth. Let all paints dry thoroughly.

Napkins & Napkin Rings
1. Spread tacky glue evenly over all surfaces of wooden napkin rings; cover with strip of coordinating fabric.

2. Launder napkins in warm water using mild soap; do not use fabric softener.

3. Follow step 2 for Place Mats. Using photo as a guide and following iron-on adhesive manufacturer's instructions, fuse pieces in place in corner of napkin: a small and medium tree, then snowman, hat, jacket, scarf, mittens and star.

4. Follow steps 4–7 for Place Mats. Fold napkin in quarters with design on top; insert center point through napkin ring.

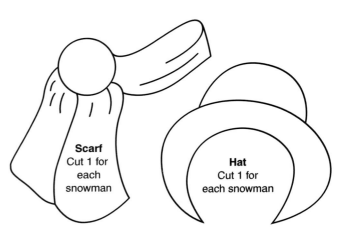

Scarf
Cut 1 for
each snowman

Hat
Cut 1 for
each snowman

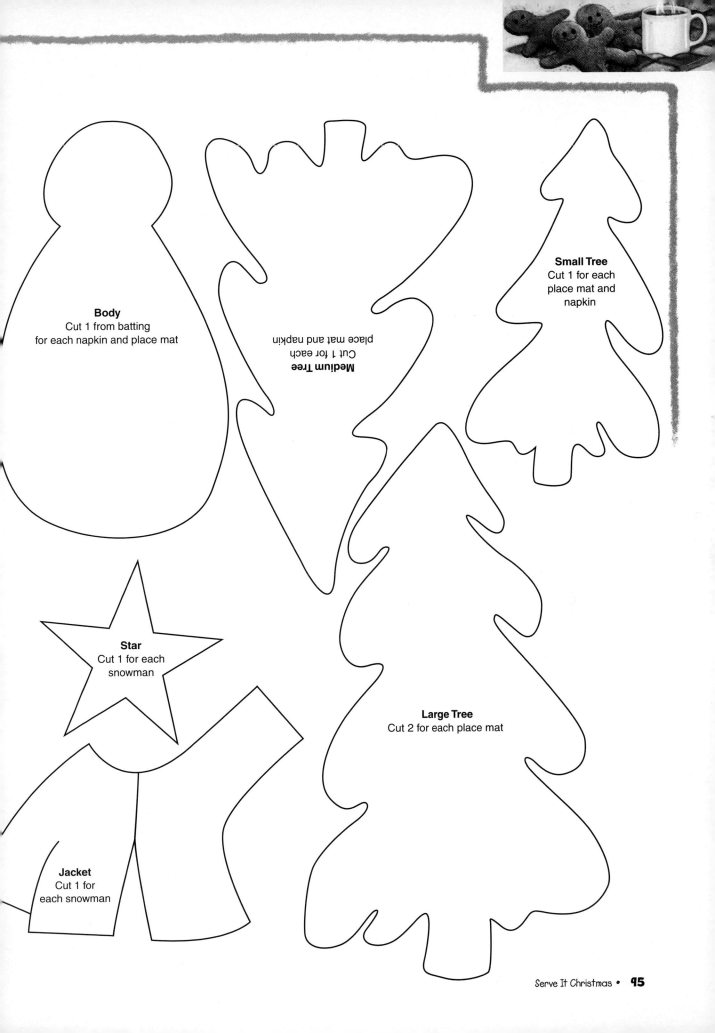

Body
Cut 1 from batting
for each napkin and place mat

Medium Tree
Cut 1 for each
place mat and napkin

Small Tree
Cut 1 for each
place mat and
napkin

Star
Cut 1 for each
snowman

Large Tree
Cut 2 for each place mat

Jacket
Cut 1 for
each snowman

Give It Christmas
Creative Handcrafted Gifts

rafters have such an advantage over noncrafters when it comes to giving great, personal gifts and saving money during the holidays! This collection of holiday gifts and stockings will give you more than a dozen sure-to-be-appreciated ideas to fill out your gift list.

Wish your little one a meowry-merry Christmas with this adorable puppet purse! Your little girl will fall in love with this kitty's soft body and expressive face. Make just one or a dozen for all the little ones on your gift list!

Christmas Kitten Puppet Purse

Design by Debi Schmitz

Materials

- *⅓ yard or 18" x 22½" craft cut white Rainbow Plush Felt from Kunin Felt*
- *⅓ yard Christmas-print fabric*
- *1 pair 42mm comical eyes from Fibre-Craft Materials Corp.*
- *Black 21mm animal nose from Fibre-Craft Materials Corp.*
- *2 (¾") silver jingle bells*
- *1 yard HeatnBond Lite iron-on adhesive from Therm O Web*
- *1 skein red #999 DMC #5 pearl cotton*
- *#20 chenille sharp needle*
- *1 pair 1" Velcro hook-and-loop fastener squares*
- *Fabri Tac permanent washable craft glue from Beacon Chemical/Signature Mktg. & Mfg.*
- *Steam iron*

Project Notes

Refer to photo throughout.

Using photocopier, enlarge patterns as directed before cutting.

All stitching is done with red #5 pearl cotton.

Instructions

1. Launder and dry print fabric without using fabric softener; steam-press. Fuse iron-on adhesive to back of fabric.

2. Referring to patterns (page 100), cut the following from adhesive-backed fabric: one purse form (complete pattern), two small eyelids, two 2" circles for cheeks, and one strip, ½" x 24", for handle.

3. From felt cut one head (cutting along dotted line on purse form pattern), two large eyelids, two 3" circles for cheeks, two ears, and two tails, reversing one.

4. Fuse fabric purse form to wrong side of remaining felt; using fabric as pattern, cut purse form from felt. Fuse adhesive-backed circles to wrong side of felt circles, centering them; fuse adhesive-backed eyelids to wrong side of felt eyelids, centering them.

5. Referring to photo and Fig. 1, glue centers of cheeks to felt head. Glue nose and eyes in place. Glue centers of eyelids in place, overlapping eyes. Blanket-stitch around cheeks and curved edges of eyelids.

6. To make whiskers, bring threaded needle out from under nose; make single long straight stitch out to side. Take a small stitch under fabric and come up at outer point of next whisker; stitch back to nose; take a tiny stitch. Repeat to make a total of four whiskers on each side and single vertical stitch for mouth.

7. Run gathering stitch along longest edge of one ear; pull to gather ear to 2½". Pin ear to head with smoother side of felt facing front; blanket-stitch ear to head along gathered edge only; continue blanket-stitch around ear, leaving remaining sides of ear free. Repeat with other ear.

8. Fold straight end of felt head to front ½"; blanket-stitch along edge to hold fold in place.

9. Blanket-stitch along straight end of fabric-backed purse form. Pin felt head to purse form, matching curved edges, with wrong side of head against felt side of purse form. Fold up straight end of purse form (see dashed line on pattern) so fabric faces fabric; pin to secure. Stitching through all layers, blanket-stitch sides of purse and around head, from one folded edge to the other.

10. Fuse ½" x 24" adhesive-backed fabric strip to wrong side of remaining felt; cut out strip and blanket-stitch around it. Stitch strap to purse, concealing ends under fold at top of head.

11. Pin felt tails together; blanket-stitch around edges. Stitch to center of turned edge on back of purse without stitching pocket shut.

12. Glue half of 1" square fastener to wrong side of head under mouth; glue other half to corresponding spot on felt for purse closure.

13. Tear 9" x 2" strip of unbacked fabric; fold into tube, wrong sides facing. Gather center tightly with #5 pearl cotton to make a bow; thread on jingle bell and stitch bow to base of tail. Repeat with a 7" x 2" strip; stitch bow with jingle bell between ears (do not stitch through the puppet—just the fabric flap). To work puppet, insert hand up back flap and work head. ✂

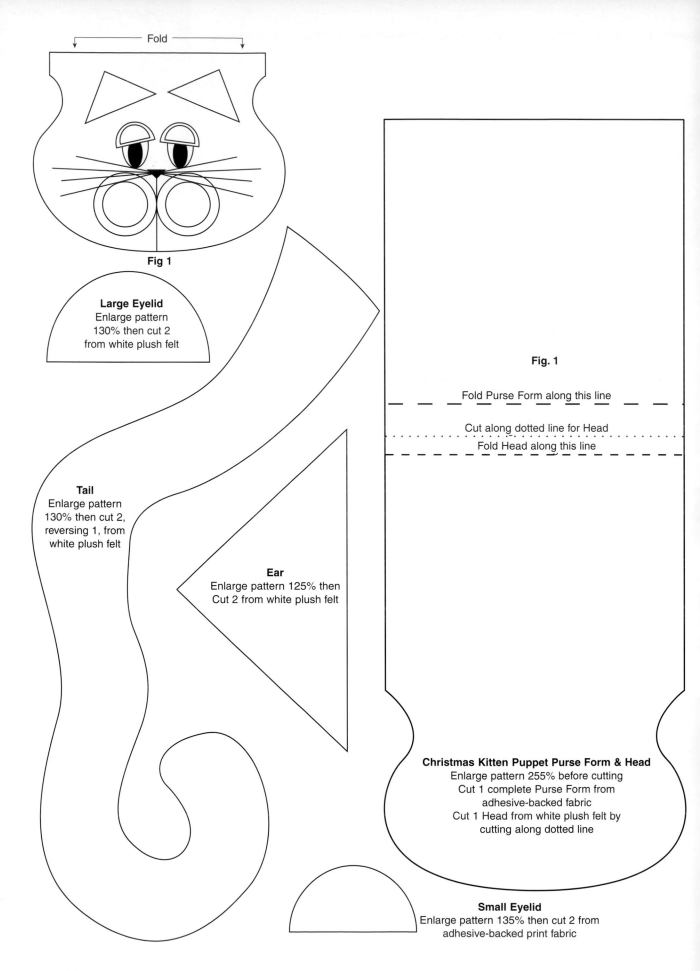

Fold

Fig 1

Large Eyelid
Enlarge pattern
130% then cut 2
from white plush felt

Tail
Enlarge pattern
130% then cut 2,
reversing 1, from
white plush felt

Ear
Enlarge pattern 125% then
Cut 2 from white plush felt

Fig. 1

Fold Purse Form along this line

Cut along dotted line for Head
Fold Head along this line

Christmas Kitten Puppet Purse Form & Head
Enlarge pattern 255% before cutting
Cut 1 complete Purse Form from
adhesive-backed fabric
Cut 1 Head from white plush felt by
cutting along dotted line

Small Eyelid
Enlarge pattern 135% then cut 2 from
adhesive-backed print fabric

E mbellish an old-fashioned box with appliqués of silk ribbon embroidery, and create a future heirloom!

Project Note

Any box with a recessed opening will do. For a smaller box, choose smaller ribbon appliqués and narrower braid trim. For larger openings, choose larger appliqués or a combination of several smaller ones and larger braid trim.

Instructions

1. Place lightweight paper over box top. Trace opening; cut out.

2. Place paper pattern on cardboard. Trace again; cut out cardboard. Slip cardboard into opening to check fit, trimming as necessary.

3. Place cardboard on fabric; trace with air-soluble pen. Referring to photo throughout, plan placement of appliqués within outline.

4. Cut out fabric ½" larger than traced shape all around.

5. Place cardboard on batting; trace and cut two shapes from batting.

6. Stack batting pieces atop cardboard. Center fabric over batting, wrong side facing batting. Smoothly wrap fabric edges around to back; glue with glue gun.

7. Apply craft cement over cardboard and fabric edges. Press into opening in box; let dry.

8. Referring to photo and using fabric glue throughout, glue braid trim around outside of opening; glue silk ribbon appliqués in place. Embellish with brass charms, stitching them to appliqués with tiny stitches. 🖉

Vintage Treasure Box

Design by Beth Wheeler

Materials

- *Simply Stitches silk-ribbon–embroidery appliqués from Westwater Enterprises*
- *Box with opening in lid (sample has opening of 3″ x 4½″)*
- *Coordinating braid trim*
- *Brass charms (sample uses a 1″ heart and ⅝″ cupid)*
- *Cardboard (sample is 3½″ x 5½″)*
- *Polyester batting*
- *Fabric for background (sample is 3½″ x 5½″)*
- *Air-soluble marking pen*
- *Low-temperature glue gun*
- *Craft cement*
- *Fabric glue*
- *Sewing needle*
- *Thread to coordinate with appliqués*

One glorious night
So long ago
In a plain and simple stall
Came a gentle message
From one so loved
Goodwill on earth
And peace to all

Love the look of cross-stitch but don't have the time to complete a large project? This inspirational pillow carries a message that is quick to stitch and a pleasure to share.

Stitch Count
91 W x 105 H

Design Size
Stitched Design:
6½" W x 7½" H

Finished Pillow:
12" W x 13⅛" H

Project Note
To stitch with variegated floss, cut an 18" length of floss; remove 2 strands. Separate these 2 strands and place their opposite ends together; thread onto needle and stitch as usual. Repeat with other strands as needed.

Stitching
1. Tape edges of fiddler's cloth or treat with seam sealant and let dry to prevent raveling. With 15" edges of fiddler's cloth at

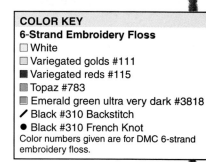

One Glorious Night Pillow
91 holes x 105 holes

COLOR KEY
6-Strand Embroidery Floss
☐ White
☐ Variegated golds #111
■ Variegated reds #115
☐ Topaz #783
☐ Emerald green ultra very dark #3818
╱ Black #310 Backstitch
● Black #310 French Knot
Color numbers given are for DMC 6-strand embroidery floss.

One Glorious Night Pillow

Design by
Sharon Barrett

Materials

- *15" x 18" 14-count fiddler's cloth*
- *DMC 6-strand embroidery floss as listed in color key*
- *Tapestry needle*
- *½ yard 36"-wide cardinal red felt*
- *Sewing threads to match fiddler's cloth and felt*
- *Fiberfill*
- *1 yard ⅝"-wide forest green satin ribbon*
- *Tape or liquid seam sealant*

top and bottom, match center of fabric to center of cross-stitch graph; begin stitching here.

2. Using 2 strands floss, cross-stitch design as graphed.

3. Using 1 strand black, backstitch as graphed. Dot i's in lettering and make dove's eye with French knots.

Assembly

1. When stitching is complete, trim fiddler's cloth so that stitching is centered in

a piece measuring 8½" W x 9⅝" H. Turn under outer edges of fiddler's cloth ½" (seven rows).

2. Cut two pieces of felt, each measuring 13" W x 14⅛" H.

3. Center fiddler's cloth right side up on right side of one piece of felt; baste layers together. Machine-stitch fiddler's cloth to felt, stitching close to fabric edge. Remove all basting stitches.

4. With right side of pillow front facing right side of pillow back and with fabric edges even, machine-stitch pillow front to back using ½" seam allowance and leaving an opening at bottom for turning. Clip corners.

5. Turn pillow cover right side out; stuff with fiberfill. Slipstitch opening closed by hand.

6. Tie ribbon in a bow; tack center of bow at upper right corner of fiddler's cloth. Trim bow ends as desired.

Pearls & Holly Gift Set

Designs by Vivian Holland-Medina

Materials

Basket

- Small basket with handle, 4" in diameter x 6" tall
- 1 package metallic gold narrow braid
- 6–8 small metallic gold poinsettias and/or holly clusters

Picture Frame

- 5" x 7" papier-mâché picture frame with 3½" x 5" opening
- Miniature gold bead garland
- 13–15 small metallic gold poinsettias and/or holly clusters

Both Projects

- Pearl bead Christmas tree garland
- Hot-glue gun

Project Note

Refer to photo throughout.

Instructions

Basket

1. Glue strand of pearls over handle to edge of basket.

2. Apply glue to body of basket and wrap strand of pearls around and around, covering basket evenly, including top edge. Check base to make sure basket stands securely.

3. Glue clusters of metallic gold poinsettias and/or holly leaves to rim of basket and where handle joins basket.

4. Wrap gold braid around handle, between individual pearls, dotting on tiny amounts of glue to secure as needed; tie braid in bows at base of handle.

Picture Frame

1. Glue miniature gold bead trim around opening in picture frame; trim as needed for even fit.

2. Winding pearl strands around and around opening, cover face of frame with pearls; cover edges of frame as well.

3. Glue clusters of metallic gold poinsettias and/or holly leaves to frame front. On sample, a cluster of about eight poinsettias is arranged in bottom right corner and extends up side; several other single poinsettias and holly clusters are glued around sides of frame.

This beautiful barrette is a gift you'll want to open *before* Christmas morning!

Christmas Carol Barrette

Design by Judi Kauffman

Materials

- 3½" barrette blank
- 3" barrette back
- 2 grape clusters from Jesse James & Co.
- Ribbon rosettes from Jesse James & Co.: 1 burgundy, 2 ivory
- Flower stamens: red and black
- Tacky craft glue
- 4" x 2" piece burgundy or deep rose synthetic suede
- Hot-glue gun

1. Apply a thin layer of tacky craft glue to curved top of barrette blank; lay it face-down on wrong side of synthetic suede. Trim off synthetic suede, leaving ½" all around. Clip curves at ends.

2. Apply glue to edges of synthetic suede and turn under. Glue barrette back in place. Allow to dry.

3. Turn barrette so curved side is up. Referring to photo throughout, glue a grape cluster at each end.

4. Cut flower stamens ½"–1" long. Glue clusters of four or five stamens so that they extend over sides of barrette, ½" from each grape cluster.

5. Glue rosettes in center of barrette, burgundy in center and ivory on each side, covering ends of wires from stamens. Let dry thoroughly before wearing.

Project Notes

Refer to photo throughout.

Enlarge patterns as indicated before cutting.

Instructions

1. Fuse transfer web to backs of tan, red pin-dot, green print and gold lamé fabrics. Referring to patterns (page 107 and 108), cut boots and other pattern pieces from fabrics as indicated.

2. Position designs on boot fronts; fuse in place.

3. With sewing machine set for narrow, slightly open zigzag stitch, machine-appliqué around all fused shapes using matching threads.

4. Cut three boot fronts from fusible fleece; fuse one to wrong side of each boot front.

5. Lay bandanna-fabric lining pieces on denim boots, right sides facing. Stitch along top edges from dot to dot as indicated on boot pattern; turn right side out and press top edges.

6. Sew one button to coyote for eye, and three to each cactus flower.

7. Stack boot fronts to backs, right sides facing. Pin in place, catching all layers on sides and bottom.

If Santa is more likely to come riding in on a horse at your house rather than be pulled by reindeer in a sleigh, these stockings are just for you! When he sees these boots waiting for him, he'll say, "Whoa!" and leave you lots of good grub!

of concha center; trim bias tape ends on an angle and treat with seam sealant; let dry. Repeat with remaining bias tape and conchas and other boots.

9. Cut 4" length of navy ribbon; fold in half for hanging loop and hand-stitch inside boot at back corner. Repeat with remaining ribbon and boots.

Cowboy Boot Stockings

Designs by Charlyne Stewart

Materials
For All Stockings

- ¾ yard lightweight denim
- ¾ yard bandanna-print fabric
- ¼ yard red fabric with metallic gold pin dots
- ¼ yard green fabric with metallic gold stars
- ¼ yard tan fabric
- 4" square gold lamé
- Matching sewing threads
- 1 spool metallic gold sewing thread from Coats & Clark
- ½ yard Pellon Wonder-Under transfer web
- 1 package fusible fleece
- 3 (1") round bronze conchas
- 7 (¼") white baby buttons
- 1 package green single-fold ½" bias tape
- ⅜ yard ¼"-wide navy grosgrain ribbon
- Seam sealant
- Sewing machine with zigzag stitch and open-toe foot
- Iron

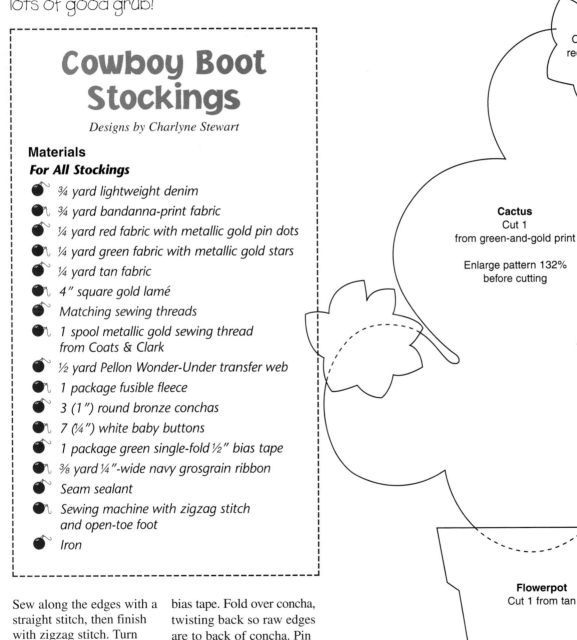

Flower
Cut 2 from red-and-gold pin-dot

Cactus
Cut 1 from green-and-gold print

Enlarge pattern 132% before cutting

Flowerpot
Cut 1 from tan

Sew along the edges with a straight stitch, then finish with zigzag stitch. Turn right side out.

8. Cut 6" length of green bias tape. Fold over concha, twisting back so raw edges are to back of concha. Pin to corner of each boot; hand-stitch on bottom edge

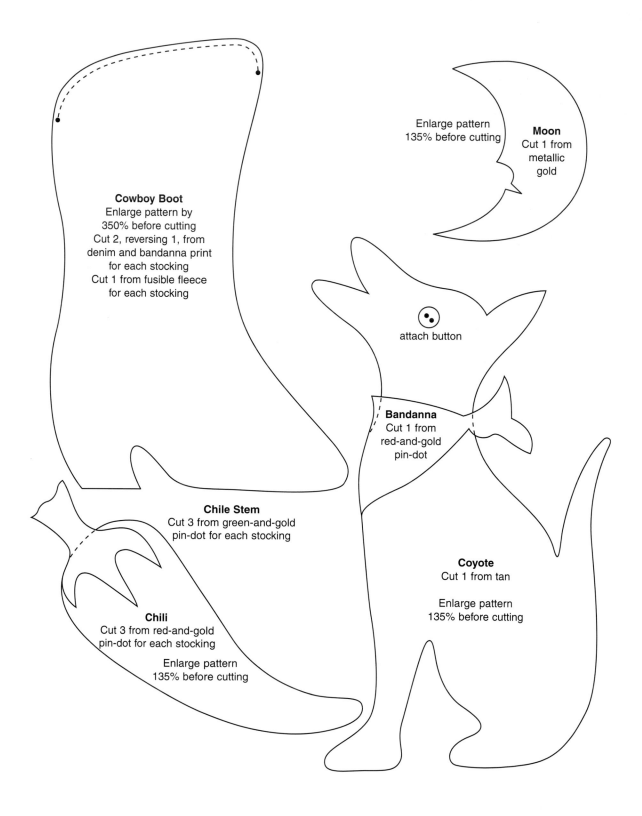

Cowboy Boot
Enlarge pattern by
350% before cutting
Cut 2, reversing 1, from
denim and bandanna print
for each stocking
Cut 1 from fusible fleece
for each stocking

Enlarge pattern
135% before cutting

Moon
Cut 1 from
metallic
gold

attach button

Bandanna
Cut 1 from
red-and-gold
pin-dot

Chile Stem
Cut 3 from green-and-gold
pin-dot for each stocking

Coyote
Cut 1 from tan

Enlarge pattern
135% before cutting

Chili
Cut 3 from red-and-gold
pin-dot for each stocking

Enlarge pattern
135% before cutting

Need a handcrafted stocking in a hurry? This large stocking is a breeze to decorate and has room for lots of goodies!

Stardust Stocking

Design by Debbie Williams

Materials

- *Red stocking with plaid cuff #1118 from BagWorks, Inc.*
- *Metallic gold #90-201-0059 Stencil Magic Stencil Paint Creme by Delta Technical Coatings, Inc.*
- *Stencil Magic stencil brushes by Delta Technical Coatings, Inc.:*
  ⅝" #98-302-0008
  ¼" #98-300-0008
- *String of stars #95-113-0012 Stencil Magic Pre-Cut Stencil by Delta Technical Coatings, Inc.*
- *14K gold #02-604 Ceramcoat Gleams paint by Delta Technical Coatings, Inc.*
- *Old toothbrush*
- *Red sewing thread and hand-sewing needle*
- *5 (10mm) gold jingle bells*
- *Freezer paper*
- *Masking tape*
- *Craft stick (optional)*
- *Steam iron*

Project Note

Refer to photo throughout.

Preparation

1. Press out any wrinkles in stocking with warm iron; laundering is not necessary. Turn stocking wrong side up and place on dull side of freezer paper; trace. Cut out stocking shape.

2. Turn fabric stocking right side up. Place freezer paper shiny side up inside stocking to keep paint from bleeding through. Secure stocking to portable work surface.

3. Cover "string" areas with masking tape on both sides of stencil, leaving only stars exposed.

4. Remove film from paint creme by placing the corner of a folded paper towel firmly on the surface of the paint and twisting as if unscrewing a jar lid. A dry film of paint will peel off; discard it.

Stenciling

1. When stenciling, use only a very little paint on a dry brush that is appropriately sized for the stencil opening. Touch brush to paint creme and press lightly. Blot any excess paint on paper towel by pressing brush in circular motion.

2. Begin by positioning stencil lengthwise down center of stocking. Firmly holding stencil in place, use stencil brushes to apply paint creme to each star in a circular motion.

3. Randomly fill remaining areas with stars, repositioning stencil as needed. If paint creme is accidentally applied in an unwanted area, press sticky side of a piece of masking tape over unwanted paint one or more times until paint is removed.

4. Place stocking on well-protected work surface. Turn cuff up so it is wrong side out; mask cuff with a piece of cardboard or freezer paper.

5. Thin a little paint slightly with water. Load old toothbrush with thinned paint and hold it over stocking. Using your thumb or a craft stick, scrape the toothbrush bristles to achieve a spattering effect. When desired look is achieved, let dry.

Finishing

1. Using red sewing thread and needle, hand-sew jingle bells to edge of stocking cuff, spacing them evenly across front and stitching only on inside layer of cuff, about 1/16" from edge. Clip loose threads.

2. No heat-setting is required; however, wait at least 10 days before laundering stocking. To launder, wash by hand using cold water and mild soap; line-dry.

Holiday Mouse Pads

Designs by Barbara A. Woolley

Materials
- Computer mouse pad
- 10" square holiday print fabric
- 10" square HeatnBond iron-on adhesive by Therm O Web
- 10" square iron-on vinyl by Therm O Web
- Press cloth
- Steam iron

You'll want to share your holiday spirit with friends and co-workers at the office, and these cheery mouse pads are just the way to do it!

1. Following manufacturer's instructions, affix iron-on adhesive to back of fabric.

2. Trace outline of mouse pad onto paper side of adhesive-backed fabric. Cut out.

3. Peel paper backing from iron-on adhesive; fuse adhesive-backed fabric to top of mouse pad.

4. Trace outline of mouse pad onto wrong side of iron-on vinyl. Cut out.

5. Following manufacturer's instructions, fuse iron-on vinyl over fabric on mouse pad.

Tack those last-minute shopping lists to your fridge with this cheery magnet. Scraps of fabric and buttons add a charming country touch. If desired, glue a pin back to it for a cute holiday accessory.

Country Christmas Tree Magnet

Design by E. Wayne Fox

Materials

- 2¼" wooden Christmas tree shape #CO-2125 by Woodworks
- ½" wooden spool #SP-4000 by Woodworks
- Woodsies ¾" wooden star by Forster Inc.
- 4" piece of 18-gauge dark annealed wire #WR-1850 by Woodworks
- 3 assorted ⅜"–½" flat buttons
- Green 6-strand embroidery floss
- 1" square of Peel n Stick double-sided adhesive by Therm O Web
- 1" square of fabric
- Verdigris #16734 Anita's Faux Easy Glaze by Plaid Enterprises, Inc.
- Americana acrylic paints from DecoArt: Sable brown #DA61 Yellow light #DA144
- Black fine-tip permanent marking pen
- Wood drill with 1/16" bit
- Craft glue
- ¼" flat paintbrush
- 1" pin back or small round magnet

Project Note

Refer to photo throughout.

Instructions

1. Drill hole through center bottom of tree, ⅛" from bottom edge.

2. Paint tree on all surfaces with verdigris glaze; paint star with yellow and spool with sable brown. Let dry.

3. Push wire through hole in tree from front until ¼" extends from back. Bend both ends down and angle them in toward one another. Place spool on wire and push up as far as possible; using needle-nose pliers, twist end of wire into a spiral to hold spool in place.

4. Using fine-point marker, draw dashed line around outside of star; glue to top of tree.

5. Apply double-sided adhesive to wrong side of fabric; trim fabric to ½" square. Apply fabric square to tree.

6. Thread embroidery floss through button; tie a knot on front of button and trim ends to ⅛"–3/16". Repeat with remaining buttons and glue each to Christmas tree.

7. Glue pin back or magnet to back of Christmas tree.

Furry Friends Stockings

Designs by Chris Malone

Materials

Cat Stocking

- Rainbow Classic Felt from Kunin Felt:
  1 square kelly green
  1 square ruby
  1 square antique gold
  1 square butterscotch
  1 square antique white
  1 square silvery gray

- DMC 6-strand embroidery floss:
  Black #310
  Gray #647
  Gold #680
  Off-white #822

- 12" black cord or linen thread

- 8" piece ⅜"-wide ruby grosgrain ribbon

- 6" piece ⅝"-wide green grosgrain ribbon

Dog Stocking

- Rainbow Classic Felt from Kunin Felt:
  1 square kelly green
  1 square ruby
  1 square cashmere tan
  1 square walnut brown
  1 square antique white

- DMC 6-strand embroidery floss:
  Black #310
  Light brown #439
  Off-white #822

- 8" piece ⅜"-wide green grosgrain ribbon

- 6" piece ⅝"-wide ruby grosgrain ribbon

Each Stocking

- ⅜" black shank button

- 2 (5mm) black round cabochons

- Craft glue

If spoiling your cat or dog is one of your favorite hobbies, then you'll want to make him or her one of these colorful felt Christmas stockings for hanging over the mantel!

Cutting & Gluing

1. Referring to patterns (pages 113 and 114), cut pieces from felt as indicated, cutting two complete stocking shapes for each stocking.

2. Referring to photo throughout, arrange stocking cuff and other pieces *except mouse ear on cat stocking and tongue on dog stocking* on each stocking front. Apply a small amount of glue to backs of pieces to tack them in place, avoiding areas that will be stitched.

Cat Stocking

1. Using running stitch and 2 strands gold floss, stitch around cat body and legs, extending stitching up center of legs ¾". Using running stitch and 2 strands off-white floss, stitch around jowls.

2. Sew shank button between jowls for nose. Glue cabochons in place for eyes.

3. For whiskers, cut black cord or linen thread into three 4" lengths. Thread needle with all three lengths and insert in jowl on one side; run through back of stocking and out opposite jowl. Tie threads as desired.

4. Tie red ⅜"-wide ribbon in bow; trim ribbon ends in a V. Glue bow to side of cat at neck.

5. Using running stitch and 2 strands gray floss, stitch around mouse's body; backstitch curved tail. Using 2 strands black floss, add French knot eye. Glue ear to mouse, applying glue only to mouse body, not stocking.

6. Using 2 strands black

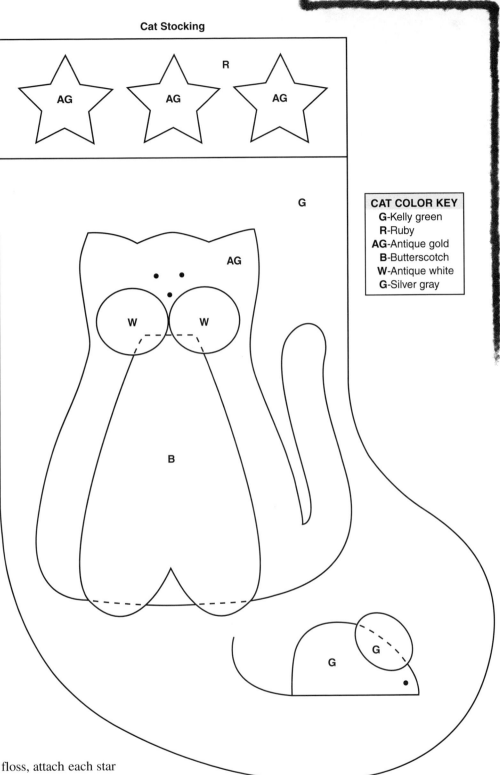

Cat Stocking

floss, attach each star through cuff and stocking front with a single short, horizontal stitch.

Dog Stocking

1. Using running stitch and 2 strands light brown floss, stitch around dog body and legs, extending stitching up center of legs ¾". Using running stitch and 2 strands off-white floss, stitch around jowls and bone. Glue tongue in place.

2. Sew shank button between jowls for nose. Glue cabochons in place for eyes.

3. Using 2 strands black floss, add three French knots to each jowl.

4. Cut a ⅜"piece from green ribbon; glue to middle of bone. Tie remainder of ribbon into a bow and glue to top of bone. Trim ribbon ends in a V.

5. Using 2 strands black floss, attach each heart through cuff and stocking front with a single short, horizontal stitch.

Finishing

1. Using 2 strands black floss, work blanket stitch across top of stocking; do not knot or clip floss.

2. Pin stocking halves together, right sides out. Fold 6" piece of ribbon in half and insert raw ends ½" into top left corner of stocking. Continue blanket stitch around stocking, catching ribbon hanger in stitches.

3. Finish by working blanket stitch across top of stocking back, leaving stocking open at top. ✏️

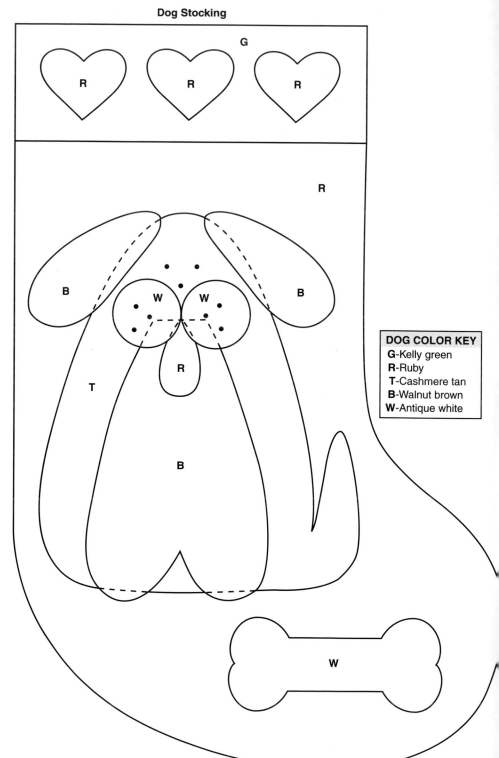

Dog Stocking

DOG COLOR KEY
G-Kelly green
R-Ruby
T-Cashmere tan
B-Walnut brown
W-Antique white

Don't forget to treat your furry friends to holiday goodies this Christmas season! These easy cross-stitch jar toppers are just right for an animal-loving friend.

Pet Treat Toppers

Designs by Mary T. Cosgrove

Materials

Both Projects

- Charles Craft Jar Lid Covers: 1 green check, 1 red check
- Madeira silk embroidery floss as listed in color key
- Tapestry needle

COLOR KEY

Silk Embroidery Floss
- ■ Red #0511
- ■ Green #1204
- ✎ Red #0511 Backstitch and Straight Stitch
- ✎ Green #1204 Backstitch

Color numbers given are for Madeira silk embroidery floss.

cross-stitch design as graphed, stitching kitty on red jar lid cover and doggy on green jar lid cover.

3. Using 2 strands floss, add backstitch and straight stitch as graphed.

4. Top jars with lid covers; embellish with ribbons or other trims as desired. ✋

Stitch Count
Doggy: 30 W x 22 H
Kitty: 22 W x 30 H

Design Size
Doggy: 2⅛" W x 1⅛" H
Kitty: 1⅛" W x 2⅛" H
Finished Toppers: 3" in diameter

Instructions
1. Count to find center of stitching area on jar lid cover; match to center of graph and begin stitching at this point.

2. Using 2 strands floss,

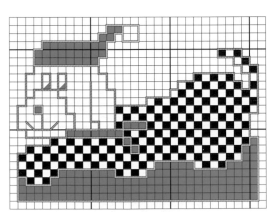

Doggy Treat Topper
30 holes x 22 holes

Kitty Treat Topper
22 holes x 30 holes

ere's a gift you'll want to give the kids before you leave for that Christmas car trip to Grandma's house! This colorful foam tic-tac-toe game will help pass the hours while spreading holiday cheer.

Instructions

1. Referring to patterns, cut four Christmas trees from green and four stars from yellow. Also cut ½" spacer squares to fit on backs of playing pieces—four yellow and four green.

2. Referring to patterns, draw outline and details on each Christmas tree and star using black fine-tip marking pen.

3. Using hole punch, punch holes in tree as indicated. Punch four circles each from yellow, red, blue, orange, pink and purple. Referring to photo, insert dots in holes in Christmas trees and glue in place.

4. Glue green spacer square to back of each tree and yellow spacer square to back of each star. Let dry.

5. Cut four 9" strips of ribbon. Glue to white craft foam to make game board. Allow pieces to dry. 🎅

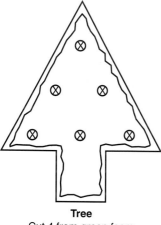

Tree
Cut 4 from green foam

Christmas Tic-Tac-Toe

Design by Helen Rafson

Materials

- Craft foam:
  9" square white
  Pieces of blue, green, red, orange, pink, purple and yellow
- Hole punch
- Black permanent fine-tip marking pen
- 1 yard ¼"-wide red ribbon
- Tacky craft glue

Star
Cut 4 from yellow foam

Fill this pretty box with your favorite potpourri, or use it as a special gift box for a close friend or family member.

Victorian Potpourri Box

Design by Susan Schultz

Materials

- 4" round papier-mâché box with lid
- Hunter green #02-471 Ceramcoat acrylic paint by Delta Technical Coatings, Inc.
- Satin-finish water-base varnish from Delta Technical Coatings, Inc.
- Robert Simmons Tole Master #12 flat paintbrush
- Cherub charm #4401 from Creative Beginnings
- Ivory crocheted doilies: 3½"–4" and 6"
- Ivory flat lace trim:
  ½ yard ½"-wide
  ½ yard 1"-wide
- ⅔ yard mauve-and-green 1"-wide wire-edge ribbon
- 5 green velvet or silk leaves
- Crinkled silk roses:
  1½"–1¾" mauve
  2 (¾") mauve
  3 (1¼") ivory
- 3 small silk ivory rosebuds
- 1 cup dry potpourri mixture
- Wire cutters
- Low-temperature glue gun

Project Note

Refer to photo throughout.

Painting

1. Paint box inside and out with two coats of hunter green paint, letting paint dry thoroughly between coats.

2. Apply one light coat of varnish; let dry.

Decorating

1. Glue wider lace trim around bottom edge of box. Glue narrower lace trim around top edge of lid side. Glue smaller doily to top of lid.

2. Tie a bow with 1½" loops in center of wire-edge ribbon. Glue ribbon center toward back edge of top; create folds and turns with the ribbon tails, bringing them around outside of doily; glue ribbon tails in place where they touch lid.

3. Using wire cutters, trim stems and leaves from roses, but do not cut rosebuds yet. Arrange leaves and roses as desired. Glue down stem edge of leaves first, making sure that tips of leaves are still free to bend up, then glue roses in place. Tuck rosebuds under a leaf or rose and glue in place. Glue cherub charm between roses and leaves.

4. Glue larger doily inside box in bottom, arranging excess evenly around sides. Pour potpourri into doily-lined box.

White over gold crackle paint creates an elegant background for two small arrangements of dried flowers on this charming switch-plate cover.

Dainty Florals Switch Plate

Design by Susan Schultz

Materials
- Wooden 2-slot switch plate
- 1⅝" wooden half-flowerpot #FLMS-3 from West Coast Wood Craft Supply
- Wood sealer from Delta Technical Coatings, Inc.
- Light ivory #02-401 Ceramcoat acrylic paint by Delta Technical Coatings, Inc.
- 14K gold #02-604 Ceramcoat Gleams paint by Delta Technical Coatings, Inc.
- Ceramcoat Crackle medium by Delta Technical Coatings, Inc.
- Clear Ceramcoat Faux Finish Glaze Base by Delta Technical Coatings, Inc.
- Satin-finish acrylic spray from Delta Technical Coatings, Inc.
- Robert Simmons Tole Master #12 flat paintbrush
- Aleene's Dried Florals:
  Green wild boxwood
  Dusty rose gypsophila
  Spearmint plumosas
  Pink delphinium
- ⅓ yard fine metallic gold cord
- Wood glue
- Dragonfly charm #4700 from Creative Beginnings
- Light sandpaper
- Tack cloth
- Kitchen timer

Project Note
Refer to photo throughout.

Be careful not to clog screw holes on switch plate with any of the finishes or paints; keep holes open with a toothpick as needed.

Painting
1. Lightly sand switch plate and flowerpot; wipe with tack cloth to remove dust. Apply a light coat of sealer; let dry completely. Sand lightly and wipe off dust.

2. Apply two coats of gold paint to all surfaces of switch plate and flowerpot, front and back, letting paint dry thoroughly after each coat.

3. Using paintbrush, apply a generous, even coat of crackle medium to front of switch plate. Set timer for 20 minutes. *Note: Crackle medium should not dry; it is ready while it still looks slightly glossy and leaves a slight imprint when touched lightly. In a very dry area, the crackle medium will dry more quickly, so pay attention to the time and check it often.*

4. Mix one part light ivory paint to one part faux finish glaze base. Generously load paintbrush with mixture and apply on top of crackle base. Start on the upper left side and move quickly across to the right, always picking up more paint. Do not over-stroke, dig brush into the wood or go back over a painted area with brush, or paint will lift off. Work quickly and evenly; cracks will follow brush strokes. Let switch plate dry thoroughly.

Finishing
1. Glue gold flowerpot to lower left side of switch plate. Glue a sprig of boxwood inside pot to switch plate; add a sprig of plumosas. Glue dusty rose gypsophila in front.

2. Glue pink delphinium, taller in the back and shorter in the front, filling in the rest of the pot. Glue a small blossom near bottom of pot.

3. Tie a few sprigs of delphinium, gypsophila and greenery into a small bouquet with gold cord; glue to upper right corner of switch plate.

4. Glue dragonfly charm to switch plate centered above openings.

5. Apply two light coats of satin-finish spray to entire surface, letting finish dry between coats. ✿

Wrap It Christmas

Holiday Cards & Wrappings

This holiday, make your gift-giving extra special by giving two gifts in one by wrapping your handcrafted present in a handcrafted bag or box that can be used again and again. You'll also find a number of decorative bows and tags to dress up your special surprise even more.

You'll love crafting this dimensional gift bag and tag set! An easy-to-paint Santa is accented with fabric strips on his beard, hat and cuffs for a fun folk-art look.

Santa Gift Bag

Design by Paula Bales

Materials

- 8" x 10" brown paper sack with handles
- Scrap of paper sack
- Black medium- and fine-point permanent marking pens
- Americana acrylic paints from DecoArt:
  Sand #DA4
  Mocha #DA60
  Black #DA155
  Santa red #DA170
- Black slick paint
- Paintbrush
- Old toothbrush
- 100 percent cotton muslin
- 22-gauge wire: silver and green
- ¼"-diameter wooden dowel
- 8 (1") imitation Christmas tree light bulbs
- Natural jute twine
- Hot-glue gun
- Hole punch

Gift Bag

1. Referring to gift bag pattern (page 123), transfer design to one side of gift bag. Referring to photo and using acrylic paints, paint face with mocha, gloves with black, and hat, coat and cheeks with Santa red. Let paints dry.

2. Dot on eyes with black slick paint, using end of wooden paintbrush handle; let dry. Add tiny eye highlights using sand paint.

3. Mix a small amount of sand paint with half as much water. Dip bristles of old toothbrush in mixture; shake off excess paint. Holding the brush over the painted sack, run fingertip across ends of bristles to spatter tiny specks of paint evenly across surface of sack. Let dry completely.

4. Retrace lettering and dashed lines with fine-point marking pen; add Santa's facial features. Outline Santa with medium-point marking pen.

5. For beard, tear 3" x ½" muslin strips; referring to photo, glue strips around face. For mustache, tear two 6" x ½" strips of muslin; knot together in center and glue in place with knot centered on face for nose.

6. For a more rumpled look, wet your hand with water and randomly squeeze and scrunch

May Your Christmas shine BRIGHT!

Santa Gift Bag Pattern
Enlarge pattern 120% to return
to original size.

Name Tag

muslin strips to moisten and wrinkle fabric; let dry undisturbed, then trim as desired.

7. Tear a 1"-wide muslin strip; twist and glue to bottom of hat. Tear another 1" strip; scrunch up and glue to top of hat.

8. To make glasses, wrap silver wire around dowel;

slide wire loop off dowel, and wrap a second loop next to the first. Trim off excess wire and glue glasses to nose.

9. Thread light bulbs on green wire, adding twists and curls between lights so individual bulbs stay in place. Glue light bulbs to Santa's gloves and sack.

Name Tag

1. Referring to name tag pattern cut one light bulb shape from paper scrap.

2. Outline tag with fine-point marker; add name or message. Punch hole in top and tie name tag to gift bag handle with natural jute.

Craft this eye-catching gift box in a jiffy! It's just the right size for holding a small gift, and even stands on its own.

Santa Star Gift Box

Design by Chris Malone

Materials
- 4" papier-mâché star-shaped box
- 1" wooden half-bead
- ½" brass jingle bell
- 3" piece artificial green bough
- Red berry pick with assorted-size berries
- 10" thin gold cord
- Acrylic paints: red, black, peach
- Snow-Tex artificial snow paste by DecoArt
- Powdered cosmetic blusher
- Cotton swab
- Satin-finish varnish
- Paintbrush
- Palette knife
- Toothpicks
- Hot-glue gun

Project Note
Refer to photo throughout for placement.

Painting
1. Paint box top and bottom, inside and out, with two coats of red paint, allowing paint to dry between coats.

2. Using black, paint "boots" and "mittens" on box top: For "boots," paint ¾" on tops and sides of two adjacent star points; for "mittens," paint ½" on tops and sides of opposing star points. Let dry.

3. Paint wooden half-bead with peach paint for Santa's head. Let dry.

4. Using tip of paintbrush handle or wooden toothpick, paint two black dots on Santa's head for eyes, and one red dot for nose; let dry. Apply cosmetic blusher to Santa's cheeks with cotton swab.

Finishing
1. Glue half-bead to box top 1" down from center of top star point. Apply satin varnish to box top and bottom, inside and out, and head.

2. Using palette knife, apply artificial snow paste to head and box top, shaping a beard and hair and covering all edges of half-bead. Use toothpick to shape a mustache under Santa's nose. Let dry.

3. Glue bell to top point of star. Curve bough; glue to one hand. Cut berries from pick; glue randomly to bough. Tie thin gold cord into a small bow and knot ends; glue bow to bough.

Project Note

Refer to photo throughout.

Instructions

1. Place large paper bag inside canvas tote; lay tote flat.

2. Squeeze a large pool of green paint onto waxed paper. Dip bath body puff or sponge into paint; blot off excess. Using a clockwise circular motion, sponge a wreath of connecting circles on front of tote. Using paintbrush, add freehand semicircles to define edges of wreath. Add additional painted details to wreath as desired. Set aside until paint is completely dry.

3. Tie ribbon in 6"-wide bow with 2¾" loops and 3¾" tails.

4. Using a doubled length of red embroidery floss, tack center of bow to top center of wreath. Tack pompoms to wreath. 🎅

You'll find many uses for this handy tote bag during the holidays. Use it for carrying gifts from the car to the house, or for your personal toting while Christmas shopping.

Christmas Wreath Tote Bag

Design by Mary T. Cosgrove

Materials

- Natural canvas open tote #0100 from BagWorks, Inc.
- Kelly green #02-052 Ceramcoat acrylic paint from Delta Technical Coatings, Inc.
- 3" sponge circle or bath body puff
- 1 yard 2½"-wide red print Christmas ribbon
- 5 (½") red pompoms
- Small paintbrush
- Waxed paper
- Large, heavy paper bag
- Christmas red 6-strand embroidery floss

Trim your tree with this set of four gift boxes! A clothespin glued to the back makes them easy to "hang."

Ornament Boxes

Designs by Bonnie Stephens

Materials

- 3" papier-mâché boxes from DC & C:
  2 square
  2 round
- Wooden cutouts from Woodworks:
  2 (1¼") mittens
  2" stocking
  1½" small heart
  2⅛" tree
  2¼" snowman
- 4 wooden spring-type clothespins
- Aleene's Premium-Coat acrylic paints:
  White #OC-173
  Black #OC-176
  Holiday red #OC-180
  Holiday green #OC-181
  Blush #OC-183
  Navy #OC-187
- Aleene's Enhancers paint products:
  All-purpose primer #EN-104
  Matte varnish #EN-107
- Tacky craft glue
- 12" x ¼" strip Christmas or country plaid fabric
- 12" jute twine
- Paintbrushes: spatter brush, ¾" flat, #10/0 liner and small round
- Sandpaper
- Transfer paper
- Stylus

Project Notes

Only exterior surfaces of boxes are primed and painted.

Refer to photo throughout for placement.

Instructions

1. Using ¾" flat brush, apply all-purpose primer to wooden cutouts, boxes and lids; let dry and sand lightly.

2. Using ¾" flat brush, paint boxes, clothespins and wooden cutouts as follows:

Mitten Box: Paint one mitten, clothespin and round box with red. Reverse other wooden mitten; paint mitten and edge of box lid green. Paint top of lid white.

Snowman Box: Paint clothespin, round box and top of lid with navy. Paint edge of box lid red. Paint tree cutout green and snowman white.

Stocking Box: Paint clothespin and square box white. Paint top of lid red. Paint stocking and edge of lid green.

Santa Box: Paint clothespin, square box and top of box lid green. Paint edge of box lid red. Referring to pattern below, paint heart cutout for Santa's face, using blush for face, red for hat and white for beard and fur trim on hat.

3. Add painted details to boxes:

Mitten Box: Using thinned black paint and liner brush, add cuff details to both mittens, and draw squiggly line around top of box lid.

Snowman Box: Using stylus, dot tiny black eyes onto snowman, redipping after each dot so eyes will be the same size. Repeat to make buttons, making buttons slightly larger than eyes. Using liner brush and red, add carrot nose.

Stocking Box: Using thinned black paint and liner brush, add cuff, heel and toe details to stocking, and draw stitching line around top of box lid.

Santa Box: Using stylus, dot tiny black eyes onto Santa, redipping after each dot so eyes will be the same size. Using small round brush and a scant amount of red paint, add cheeks. Using small round brush, paint a second layer of fur trim on Santa's hat and add white pompom at top. Using liner brush and white, paint "Ho Ho Ho" on box lid.

4. Glue mittens to mitten box lid and tree to left side of snowman box lid.

5. Using thinned white paint and spatter brush, lightly spatter boxes and lids for snowman and Santa boxes, mitten box and stocking box lid. Spatter base of stocking box and mitten box lid with thinned red, then thinned green. Allow to dry.

6. Glue flat side of clothespin to bottom of each box. Glue stocking to stocking box lid, snowman to right side of snowman box lid and Santa to Santa box lid. Let dry thoroughly.

7. Apply one or two coats of matte varnish to lids, boxes and clothespins; let dry between coats.

8. Cut fabric strip in two; tie each half with knot in center. Glue one to stocking top and one to snowman for scarf; trim ends as desired.

9. Cut jute twine in two; tie each half in simple bow. Glue one atop mittens and one below Santa's chin; trim ends as desired.

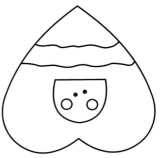

Ornament Boxes Santa

Nature's Gift Bows

Designs by Creative Chi

Materials

Burgundy Bow

- 24" 1½"-wide gold-edged wired burgundy velveteen ribbon
- Botanicals from Creative Chi:
  2 salal leaves
  2 bay leaves
  4 red milo berry sprigs
  3 white milo berry sprigs
  4 lunaria
  Pecan
  4 hemlock cones
  4 jackie berries

Red Bow

- 24" 1½"-wide gold-edged wired red velveteen ribbon
- Botanicals from Creative Chi:
  3 boxwood sprigs
  4 bay leaves
  3 lunaria
  3 white milo berry sprigs
  3 filberts
  3 hemlock cones

Green Bow

- 24" 1½"-wide gold-edged wired green velveteen ribbon
- Botanicals from Creative Chi:
  2 salal leaves
  4 cedar tips
  Dried apple slice
  4 eucalyptus leaves
  2 red milo berry sprigs
  2 almonds
  2 birch cones
  3 jackie berries

Each Bow

- 9" 20-gauge green florist wire
- 1½" Woodsie wooden round disk from Forster Inc.
- True gold #DG37 Ultragloss Metallic acrylic paint from DecoArt
- Small paintbrush
- Low-temperature glue gun

D ress up a gift with one of these beautiful velvet gift bows decorated with a variety of dried nuts, berries, leaves and pinecones.

Project Note

Refer to photo throughout for placement.

Instructions

1. Referring to lists of botanicals needed for each bow, gild the following by brushing with metallic gold paint:

Burgundy Bow: Gild bay leaves, pecan and hemlock cones.

Red Bow: Gild bay leaves, filberts and hemlock cones.

Green Bow: Gild salal leaves, cedar tips, dried apple slice, eucalyptus leaves, almonds and birch cones.

2. Form bow from wired ribbon; wrap 20-gauge wire around center to secure.

3. Glue sprigs of foliage to wooden circle to form background; add cones or nuts in center. Fill in with remaining botanicals.

4. Glue decorated wooden circle to center of bow.

Tuck a special jewelry gift inside one of these decorative boxes accented with tiny pinecones, greenery and berries.

Project Note

Refer to photo throughout.

Instructions

1. Glue pieces of ribbon across top of box lid, gluing ribbon ends to inside edges of lids.

2. Arrange and glue botanicals to top center of box lid, beginning with foliage, statice sprigs and lunaria. Add central flowers and cones; finish with berries.

Pinecone Accents Jewelry Boxes

Designs by Creative Chi

Materials

Box A

- 9″ length of ⅜″-wide red-and-white striped ribbon

- Botanicals from Creative Chi:
  2 preserved cedar tips
  2 lunaria
  3 white-frosted birch cones
  2 sprigs canella berries
  3 hemlock cones
  Strawberry globe amaranth

Box B

- 9″ length of ⅜″-wide red-and-green striped ribbon

- Botanicals from Creative Chi:
  5 German statice sprigs
  2 boxwood sprigs
  3 white-frosted birch cones
  2 hemlock cones
  8 jackie berries

Each Box

- Small natural brown kraft jewelry box

- Low-temperature glue gun

Delicate pressed flowers arranged into beautiful designs make each of these Christmas cards a special expression of goodwill and cheer.

Pressed-Flower Holiday Cards

Designs by Creative Chi

Materials

Swag Card

- Assorted pressed flowers and leaves from Creative Chi:
  3 red azalea petals
  7 pieces of fern leaves
  6 red verbena
  6 white verbena
  5 mini Queen Anne's lace florets
  Sweet Annie leaves

Wreath Card

- Assorted pressed flowers and leaves from Creative Chi:
  9–11 red verbena
  4–6 pink verbena
  6–7 mini Queen Anne's lace florets
  Sweet Annie leaves
  Tansy leaves
- 8" ¼"-wide burgundy double-face ribbon

Each Card

- Blank natural greeting card with matching envelope
- Flat tweezers with rounded edges (no sharp points)
- Matte-finish Modge Podge decoupage medium by Plaid Enterprises, Inc.
- Small paintbrush

Project Notes

Refer to photo throughout.

Dried flowers are fragile and tear easily. A pair of smooth, flat tweezers makes handling the flowers easier.

Instructions

1. To position a leaf or flower, paint a small amount of decoupage medium on card where flower is to be placed. Carefully position flower, then cover lightly with more decoupage medium (it will dry clear) to just beyond the edge of the flower.

2. Work from back to front in layers. First apply the background leaves and flowers. Then apply medium midground flowers. Finally apply the small foreground flowers and accents.

Swag Card

1. Begin with Sweet Annie leaves, then azaleas and fern bits.

2. Add verbenas and finally the Queen Anne's lace.

Wreath Card

1. Trace a very light penciled circle approximately 3" across; use this line as a reference point to keep wreath circular. Be sure to cover line completely as you will not be able to erase it.

2. Apply tansy and Sweet Annie leaves, alternately.

3. Add verbenas and Queen Anne's lace. Tie ribbon in bow; glue to card. ✍

*I*f you occasionally send holiday cards without a Christmas motif, then you'll enjoy making and sharing this card with family and friends.

Columbia Star Card

Design by Kathy Wegner

Materials

- Strathmore Paper 5" x 6⅛" blank greeting card #105-150 or #105-120
- 6 medium Woodsies wooden diamonds from Forster Inc.
- FolkArt acrylic paints from Plaid Enterprises, Inc.:
  Violet pansy #440
  Lemon custard #735
  Glazed carrots #741
  Tapioca #903
  Christmas red #958
- Apple Barrel paints from Plaid Enterprises, Inc.:
  Periwinkle blue #20769
  Green clover #20776
- Paintbrush
- Fine-point black permanent marking pen
- Matte-finish varnish
- Tacky craft glue
- Waxed paper

Instructions

1. Paint each diamond a different color using each color paint except tapioca. Using tapioca paint, marking pen and any of the other colors, decorate painted diamonds to resemble calico prints (refer to photo). Let dry.

2. Brush painted diamonds with matte varnish; let dry.

3. Using black marking pen, draw 4" square in center of card, drawing in a "running stitch." Referring to photo throughout, glue diamonds in star shape.

4. Cover card with a piece of waxed paper; press flat under heavy books. When flat, outline star with "running stitch," using fine-point marker.

Botanicals make classy Christmas accents. Just take a look at this pair of colorful cards! Turn out a whole stack in just an evening.

Botanical Cards

Designs by Blanche Lind

Materials

- 5" x 7" blank card stock
- Fusible webbing
- Fabric scraps in holiday botanical prints with gold highlights: poinsettias, amaryllis, holly, mistletoe, etc.
- Metallic gold marking pen

Instructions

1. Following manufacturer's instructions, fuse webbing to wrong sides of fabrics. Referring to photo throughout, cut floral motifs from fabric.

2. Position floral cutouts on front of card; fuse to card front. Let cool.

3. Using metallic gold pen, outline fabric shapes and/or sketch additional botanical accents as desired.

Pop-Up Holiday Bags

Design by Crystal Harris Ogle

Materials

- Paper gift bag with handles
- Tacky craft glue
- Foam dots with adhesive on both sides or scraps of craft foam
- Christmas cards: 2 duplicates for each design

R ecycle last year's Christmas cards by using them to make this year's gift bags!

Project Notes

Choose cards with elements or motifs that can be cut out completely. Elements from two or three cards may be combined to make one bag. Refer to photo for placement.

Instructions

1. Plan layout of design. Cut out one complete motif or figure; glue to bag where desired. Choose a portion of the motif to be in the foreground, such as a closer tree, or hands holding out an item. Cut this foreground piece from the duplicate card.

2. Place one or more adhesive foam dots on the part of complete motif that corresponds to foreground piece. Place foreground piece atop dots to give design a three-dimensional look. (To substitute craft foam for adhesive foam dots, glue two tiny foam squares together; glue to complete motif and foreground piece.)

Paper-Craft Gift Bag & Tag

Designs by Deborah Spofford

Materials

- 7" x 8½" x 4" corrugated cardboard gift bag
- 2" x 6" piece brown paper
- 4" square Paperbilities green corrugated cardboard from MPR Associates
- 2¾" x 4" piece watercolor paper
- 4" x 5" piece Paperbilities textured brown paper from MPR Associates
- 4¾" x 8¾" piece Paperbilities plaid paper from MPR Associates
- Opaque red #02-507 Ceramcoat acrylic paint from Delta Technical Coatings, Inc.
- #4 shader and #0 liner paintbrushes from Loew-Cornell
- 14" natural raffia
- 14" natural jute twine
- Fine-line permanent black marking pen
- Hole punch
- Tacky craft glue

If you can tear a piece of paper, you can craft this rustic-style gift bag and tag with the greatest of ease!

Project Note

Refer to photo throughout for placement.

Instructions

Gift Bag

1. Referring to patterns, cut one tree and one star from green corrugated cardboard. Cut two pieces of plaid paper, one 4¾" x 6¼" and one 1½" x 2¼". Tear edges of brown textured, plaid and watercolor papers.

2. Paint watercolor paper with water, then paint with red paint. Let dry.

3. Glue plaid paper to center front of bag; top with brown textured paper, then painted watercolor paper. Glue tree to watercolor paper.

4. Using #4 shader brush, paint wavy red line along top and bottom edges of gift bag; let dry.

5. Tie raffia in bow; glue to Christmas tree.

Gift Tag

1. Fold 6" x 2" brown paper in half to make 3" x 2" gift tag. Glue 1½" x 2¼" piece plaid paper to front of gift tag; glue star to plaid paper.

2. Using fine-point marking pen, draw border of dashed lines around front of gift tag.

3. Using #0 liner, paint wavy red line along top and bottom edges of tag; let dry.

4. Punch hole near center top edge of gift tag. Fold jute in half; loop it through hole and tie tag to handle of gift bag. ✿

Instructions begin
on page 136

Made from soft-to-the-touch felt, this gift bag is a cinch to make, and may be given to guys and gals alike.

1. From red felt cut two 14" squares and one 3" square.

2. Following manufacturer's instructions, apply iron-on adhesive to wrong side of green felt, tan felt and 3" square of red felt.

3. Referring to patterns, cut tree from green felt, tree trunk from tan and heart from red.

4. Position tree trunk on bottom center of bag front. Place shiny side of pressing paper down on bag front. Press for three or four seconds. Remove paper when surface is cool. Repeat with tree and heart.

5. Using 3 strands black embroidery floss, blanket-stitch around bottom and side edges of tree trunk, all edges of tree and all edges of heart.

6. Lay bag front atop back, right sides facing. Using red thread, seam bag front and back together along bottom and up sides. Clip corners; turn bag right side out. Using pressing paper, press bag.

7. Using 3 strands black embroidery floss, blanket-stitch around top edge of bag.

8. Close bag by wrapping jute twine around top and tying it.

Pine Tree Gift Bag

Design by Angie Wilhite • Shown on page 135

Materials

- *Rainbow Classic Felt by Kunin:*
  ½ yard red
  6" square pirate green
  2" x 4" piece cashmere tan
- *¼ yard HeatnBond Lite iron-on adhesive from Therm O Web*
- *HeatnBond pressing paper from Therm O Web*
- *30" thick jute twine*
- *Black 6-strand embroidery floss*
- *Tapestry needle*
- *Red sewing thread*
- *Iron*

Instructions begin on page 138

Happy Holidays Postcards

Designs by Kathy Wegner

Materials

Holly Card

- Stencil Magic Stencil Paint Cremes from Delta Technical Coatings, Inc.: Christmas red #90-122-0059 Christmas green #90-131-0059
- ¼" checkerboard stencil
- Removable tape

Christmas Tree Card

- Stencil Magic Stencil Paint Cremes from Delta Technical Coatings, Inc.: Eggnog yellow #90-101-0059 Paprika #90-123-0059 Colonial green #90-133-0059

Each Postcard

- 4" x 6" Imperial Watercolor postcard from Strathmore Paper
- Stencil Magic paintbrushes from Delta Technical Coatings, Inc.: ¼" stencil brush #98-300-0008 ⅜" Super Shader #98-351-0008
- Fine-point black marking pen
- Art gum eraser
- Stencil Magic top coat spray from Delta Technical Coatings, Inc.

These super quick-to-craft postcards make perfect Christmas cards to send to family and friends, or handy gift tags.

Project Notes

Read directions on paint package before beginning.

Practice stenciling on scrap paper before trying a postcard. Also, if using topcoat spray, test on a scrap that has been drawn on with marking pen to make sure marker doesn't run.

Blot excess paint off brushes and apply paints lightly to prevent oily halos.

Minor mistakes can often be removed with an art gum eraser.

Instructions
Holly Card

1. Referring to patterns for holly leaf and berry (page 139), trace two holly leaves and three berries onto front of card very lightly with pencil, referring to photo (page 137). Using black marking pen, mark dashed outlines around leaves and berries. Erase any visible pencil marks.

2. Place checkerboard stencil over leaves; tape stencil in place to keep paint out of unwanted areas.

3. Rub skin off top of paints with paper towel. Dab ¼" brush lightly into green paint; rub excess off onto paper towel. Brush color around outside edges of checkerboard squares, leaving centers of squares lighter. Repeat on second holly leaf.

4. Dab Super Shader lightly on red paint; blot excess off onto paper towel. Apply red to berries, carefully filling in dashed lines and leaving centers lighter.

5. Let card dry for 48 hours. Spray with topcoat if desired.

Christmas Tree Card

1. Referring to patterns for tree and star (page 139), trace tree and star onto front of card very lightly with pencil, referring to photo. Using black marking pen, mark dashed outlines around tree and star. Erase any visible pencil marks.

2. Rub skin off top of paints with paper towel. Dab ¼" brush lightly into green paint; rub excess off onto paper towel. Brush color around outside edges of tree, leaving some center areas lighter.

3. Dab clean ¼" brush lightly into yellow paint; rub excess off onto paper towel. Brush color around outside edges of star, leaving center lighter. Dab Super Shader lightly into paprika paint; blot excess off onto paper towel. Apply paprika to star tips, blending with yellow.

4. Let card dry for 48 hours. Spray with topcoat if desired.

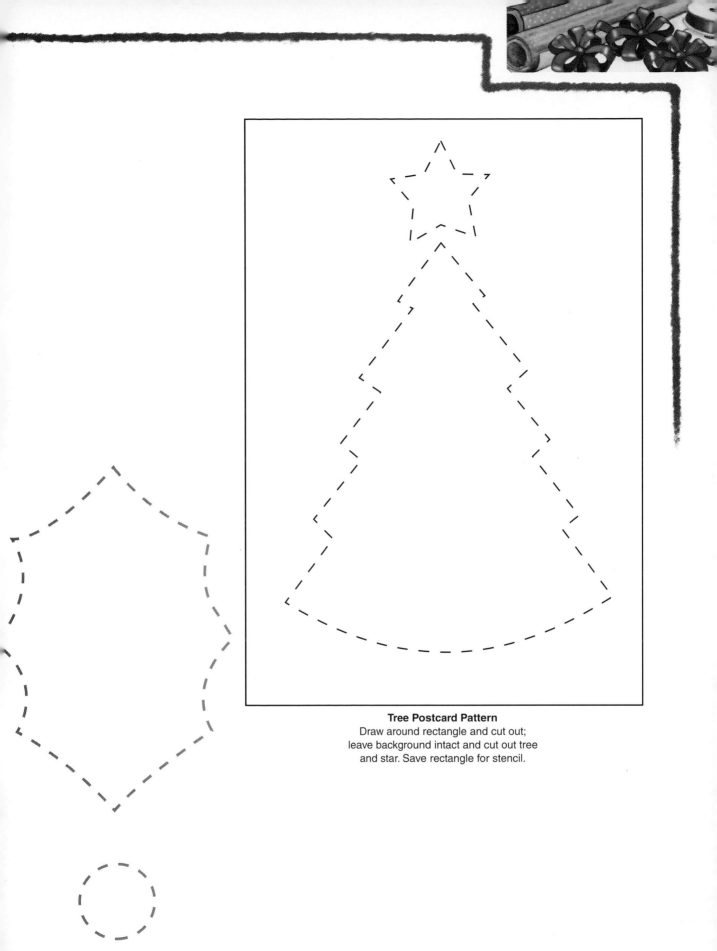

Tree Postcard Pattern
Draw around rectangle and cut out;
leave background intact and cut out tree
and star. Save rectangle for stencil.

Celebrate It
Christmas

A Cast of Holiday Characters

nvite this host of Christmas characters into your home to celebrate the holidays with fun and frivolity! Santa, Mrs. Santa, snowmen, the Three Wise Men, Rudolph and more will be a delight to craft and share!

Winter Friends Gift Pots

Designs by Delores Ruzicka

Materials

Gingerbread Boy

- Aleene's Premium-Coat acrylic paints:
  Deep peach #OC-116
  Ivory #OC-179
  Black #OC-176
  Medium red #OC-102
  Holiday red #OC-180
- Flat red button

Snowman

- Aleene's Premium-Coat acrylic paints:
  Ivory #OC-179
  Deep mauve #OC-104
  Black #OC-176
  Medium red #OC-102
  Medium poppy #OC-108
  Burnt umber #OC-185
  Deep blue #OC-152
- Aleene's True Snow artificial snow paste
- Flat blue or gray buttons:
  1 for small snowman
  2 for large snowman

Each Gift Pot

- 8" x 10" piece ¼"-thick birch stock
- Scroll saw or band saw
- Sandpaper
- Paintbrushes: #10 flat, #4 flat and #10/0 detail
- Satin varnish
- Scrap of coordinating cotton fabric
- Clay flowerpot:
  2" for smaller design
  4" for larger design
- Aleene's Designer Glue

Project Notes

Not only do these delightful characters make terrific gift caddies, but they also make whimsical table decorations!

Painting and assembly instructions are essentially the same for small and large designs.

Refer to photo for placement, letting paints dry as needed to avoid smearing or sticking.

Instructions

Gingerbread Boy

1. Referring to patterns for large and small gingerbread boys (pages 144–145), cut shape from birch stock. Sand until smooth.

2. Using #10 flat brush, base-coat all surfaces of gingerbread boy with deep peach paint, using two coats if necessary.

3. Using #10/0 detail brush and ivory, paint wavy outline around gingerbread boy. Add eyes and eyelashes in black and heart-shaped cheeks using medium red; add medium red "stitch line" for mouth. Add tiny ivory highlight dots to eyes and cheeks. Repeat ivory outline on back of gingerbread boy.

4. When paints are completely dry, coat all surfaces with satin varnish; let dry.

5. Tear strip from fabric; tie around gingerbread boy's neck in a bow. Glue button to center front of gingerbread boy.

6. Using #10 flat paintbrush, paint clay pot inside and out with holiday red; use two coats as needed to cover completely.

7. Using ivory, paint ⅝"-wide stripes on the diagonal about 1½" apart all around the pot; paint a narrow stripe on each side of each wider stripe to resemble peppermint stripes.

8. When paint is completely dry, cover pot with satin varnish.

9. Position gingerbread boy over edge of flowerpot and glue in place. Fill pot with small gifts, treats, etc.

Snowman

1. Referring to patterns for large and small snowmen (pages 144 and 146), cut shape from birch stock. Sand until smooth.

2. Using #10 flat brush, base-coat all surfaces of snowman with ivory paint, using two coats if necessary.

3. Using #4 brush, paint earmuffs and mittens with deep mauve.

4. Using #10/0 detail brush and black paint, add eyes, eyelashes, snowman outlines and details to earmuffs and mittens. Paint round cheeks using medium red; add dotted black line for mouth. Add tiny ivory highlight dots to eyes and cheeks. Paint carrot-shaped nose with medium poppy; add outline and details in black.

5. Thin burnt umber paint with water until it is the consistency of thin milk. Using #4 flat brush, float a thin coat of this mixture

around the shape of the snowman and along his neck and torso lines for shading.

6. Repeat deep mauve mittens and earmuffs, black outlining and mitten and earmuff details, and thinned burnt umber shading on back of snowman.

7. When paints are completely dry, coat all surfaces with satin varnish; let dry.

8. Daub touches of dimensional snow paint on top of snowman's head and arms.

9. Tear strip from fabric; tie around snowman's neck in a bow. Glue one button to center front of small snowman, and two buttons to large snowman.

10. Using #10 flat paintbrush, paint clay pot inside and out with deep blue; use two coats as needed to cover completely.

11. Using #10/0 detail brush and ivory, paint small snowflakes and dots randomly over surface of pot.

12. When paint is completely dry, cover pot with satin varnish; let dry.

13. Position snowman over edge of flowerpot and glue in place. Fill pot with small gifts, treats, etc.

Small Gingerbread Boy

Small Snowman

Cappuccino Mix

1 cup dry instant coffee creamer

1 cup dry instant chocolate drink mix

⅔ cup instant coffee crystals

½ cup sugar

½ teaspoon ground cinnamon

½ teaspoon ground nutmeg

Combine all ingredients; mix well. Store in an airtight container.

For each serving, stir 3 teaspoons Cappuccino Mix into 6 ounces hot water; blend well.

Large Gingerbread Boy

Large Snowman

*H*ang this delightful reindeer door hanger on your front door. Golden jingling bells on his antlers will let you know when a guest has arrived!

Jingles the Reindeer

Design by Jacqueline Bessner

Materials

- Rainbow Classic Felt from Kunin Felt:
  2" square red
  3" square white
  12" square tan
- Brown 6-strand embroidery floss
- Tapestry needle
- Sewing thread: tan and red
- Polyester fiberfill
- ½" round button for nose
- 2 (¼") round black cabochons
- 6 (¼") jingle bells
- Buttermilk #DA3 Americana acrylic paint from DecoArt
- #00 liner paintbrush from Loew-Cornell
- Cotton mop strand or yarn
- 3" x 20" strip Christmas print or plaid fabric
- Cosmetic blusher
- 20" black craft wire
- Pinking shears
- Sewing machine
- Hot-glue gun

Project Note

Refer to photo throughout for placement.

Instructions

1. Referring to patterns (page 148), cut one nose from red felt and one muzzle from white using regular scissors. Cut two ears and two heads from tan felt using pinking shears.

2. Using brown embroidery floss, hand-stitch muzzle to one head using long straight stitches as shown on pattern. Referring to Eyebrow Stitch Diagram (below), add eyebrows—each a single straight stitch between two French knots.

3. With wrong sides of fabric facing, machine-stitch head pieces together using ¼" seam allowance and leaving opening at bottom for stuffing.

4. Stuff head with fiberfill; hand-stitch opening closed.

5. Using red thread, hand-sew a gathering stitch around edge of nose. Place a small amount of fiberfill in center of felt, then lay button over stuffing and

pull gathering thread to close felt tightly around button. Knot off thread and clip ends. Hot-glue nose to face where indicated.

6. Pinch one ear at base; hot-glue to back of head where indicated. Repeat with other ear. Glue black cabochons in place for eyes; glue jingle bells to

antlers as shown in photo.

7. Using buttermilk paint and liner brush and referring to photo, add highlights to left eye; reverse design for right eye. Let paint dry.

8. Unravel cotton mop strand or yarn; cut 12 (2") pieces. Fold each in half and glue to center of forehead for bangs; trim as desired.

9. Tie fabric strip in bow; glue at neck.

10. Apply blusher to reindeer's cheeks and inside ears.

11. Curl wire ends around pencil; slip wire end off pencil and glue ends of wire to back of head. ✎

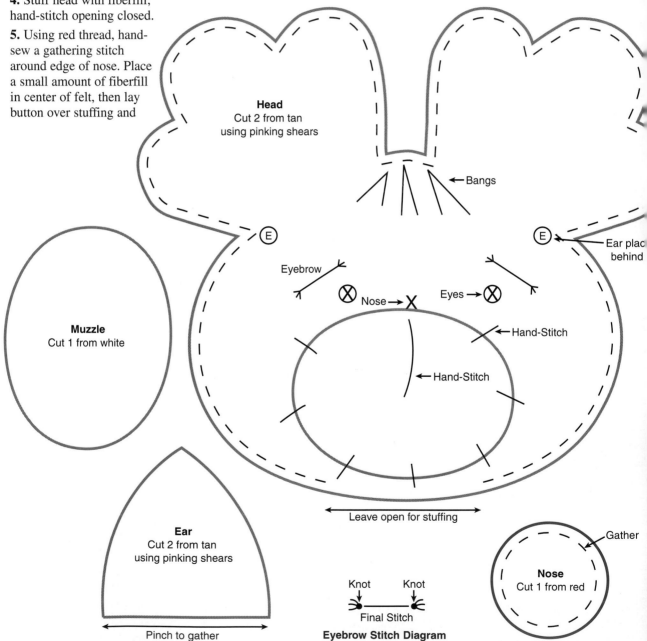

Head
Cut 2 from tan
using pinking shears

← Bangs

E

E → Ear placed behind

Eyebrow

⊗ Nose → X   Eyes → ⊗

Muzzle
Cut 1 from white

← Hand-Stitch

← Hand-Stitch

Leave open for stuffing

Ear
Cut 2 from tan
using pinking shears

Pinch to gather

Knot   Knot

Final Stitch
Eyebrow Stitch Diagram

Gather

Nose
Cut 1 from red

What goodies is Santa bringing to your house? After you craft this chummy Santa, fill his sack with Christmas candies to treat your family and friends.

Santa Centerpiece

Design by Mary Ayres • Shown on page 150

Materials

- Felt: skin tone, red and black
- 2 cardboard tubes from bathroom tissue rolls
- Strands cut from a cotton mop or cotton yarn
- Sewing thread: white, red and green
- ½" wooden furniture finishing button
- Americana acrylic paints from DecoArt:
  Toffee #DA59
  Lamp (ebony) black #DA67
  Cherry red #DA159
- Paintbrushes: #3 soft round, ¼" stencil brush and #8 round
- Black fine-line permanent marking pen
- ½" white pompom
- Scrap of white fake fur
- ½" flat metallic gold button
- 2½" wooden heart cutout
- Pinking shears
- 8" square green print fabric
- ¼ yard ⅛"-wide metallic gold braid or cord
- 3½" x 5" oval wooden plaque
- True gold #DG37 Ultra Gloss Metallic acrylic paint from DecoArt
- Craft glue

Project Note

Refer to photo for placement.

Santa

1. From skin-tone felt cut 5¾" x 4½" rectangle. Glue around cardboard tube, overlapping ends; seam will be back of Santa.

2. From red felt, cut 6¼" x 3½" rectangle; glue around bottom of same cardboard tube, overlapping edges in back.

3. For hair and beard, cut 1½" lengths from mop or yarn; separate strands. Spread glue on skin-tone felt around top edge, leaving 1" open for face. Glue yarn strands vertically around top edge for hair. With pencil, mark 1" down from top edge around face; spread additional glue just below this line. Glue yarn pieces vertically along this line to make beard. Trim ends of beard, rounding sides.

4. For mustache, cut four or five 2" strands of yarn; tie together tightly in center with white thread. Fan out strands on each side of mustache and glue to face to hide ends of beard.

5. For nose, paint wooden furniture button with toffee paint using #3 soft round brush; let dry. Dip dry ¼" stencil brush in cherry red; wipe excess paint from brush onto paper towel until brush is almost completely dry and no brush strokes are visible. Rub brush across Santa's nose and cheeks in a circular motion until desired color is achieved. Glue nose to center of face at top of beard.

6. For eyes, make two dots with permanent marking pen, positioning eyes ¼" apart and ⅛" above nose.

7. For hat, cut 2" x 6½" rectangle from red felt. Overlap short ends ¼" and glue together to make tube.

Run basting thread around one long edge close to edge; pull thread tightly to gather and knot. Glue pom-pom on top of gathered stitches for top of hat.

8. From white fur, cut ½" x 7" strip for hatband; glue around bottom edge of hat, overlapping ends in back.

9. For belt, cut 6½" x ⅜" strip from black felt. Glue around body just below beard, overlapping ends in back. Glue gold metallic button on top of belt at center front.

10. For arms, cut 8" x ½" strip from red felt; tie knot at each end for hands. Glue center of arms to center back of body just below hair.

11. For feet, paint wooden heart cutout with lamp (ebony) black. Glue heart to bottom of body with point of heart at center back.

Gift Bag

1. Cut 2" section from remaining cardboard tube. From black felt, cut 5¼" x 2⅛" rectangle and glue inside tube, overlapping ends in front.

2. Using pinking shears, cut 7" circle from green fabric. With green thread, sew gathering stitch around circle ¼" from edge. Gather stitches slightly; insert felt-lined tube into bag, and gather basting stitches around tube snugly so that pinked fabric edge is even with top edge of tube. Knot off basting thread; glue pinked fabric edges to cardboard tube.

3. Tie gold braid or cord in bow; trim ends. Glue over

basting thread at center front of bag.

Base & Assembly

1. Paint oval plaque with two or three coats cherry red paint, allowing paint to

dry between coats.

2. Dip dry #8 round brush in true gold enamel; wipe excess onto paper towel until almost dry. Wipe paint brush across top and edges of plaque until

desired color is achieved.

3. Glue Santa to left side of base, with Santa turned slightly to right. Glue bottom of bag to right side of base. Spread glue with a brush around the inside bag

fabric in areas under cardboard tube. Push cardboard tube down on top of glue and hold in place with masking tape until dry (this will keep bag stable on base to hold candy canes).

Delight the carolers who grace your home with good will and song by giving each of them one of these choir girls.

Instructions

1. Paint head bead with skin-tone paint; let dry. Referring to photo, add facial features with fine-point black marking pen. Apply a little cosmetic blusher to cheeks with fingertip.

2. For arms, cut 6" section of pipe cleaner; fold back ½" on each end for hands. Hot-glue center of pipe cleaner to doll pin.

3. For skirt, glue or sew trim to one long edge of fabric rectangle. Hand-sew gathering stitch along other long edge of rectangle. Wrap rectangle around doll pin, pull gathering thread and knot to secure; overlap will be back of doll. Clip thread ends.

4. Referring to pattern, cut one cape from crushed velvet, cutting out large circle with pinking shears and cutting out opening with scissors. Glue or sew trim around outer edge of cape.

Lay cape over singer's head so it rests on shoulders. Wrap ribbon or trim around singer's neck and hot-glue in place.

5. Hot-glue hair to singer's head as desired.

6. For hat, make a yo-yo from fabric circle by hand-sewing a running stitch along the edge, folding fabric down ¼" from the edge. Pull thread tight to make yo-yo. Glue yo-yo to singer's head like a tam; glue on pompom.

7. Paint cover of book green; let dry. Paint pages white; let dry. Using marking pen, add page lines, title to cover, etc. Decorate book covers with holly leaves painted with dimensional pearlescent light green paint; let dry. Add holly berries with dimensional red paint; let dry. Add veins to leaves with marking pen. Hot-glue book to singer's pipe cleaner hands.

Li'l Choir Girls

Design by Barbara A. Woolley

Materials

Each Choir Girl

- Doll pin with stand (clothespin and 1¼" head bead)
- Acrylic craft paints: skin tone, white and green
- Paintbrush
- Fine-line black permanent marking pen
- Powdered cosmetic blusher
- Skin-tone pipe cleaner
- Tacky glue
- Hot-glue gun
- 24" ½"-wide metallic gold trim
- Hand-sewing needle
- Coordinating sewing threads
- Coordinating Christmas-print fabric: 2" x 3" rectangle 3" circle
- 3½" square crushed velvet
- Pinking shears
- 11" 3mm-wide holiday ribbon
- Small amount of doll hair
- Coordinating 8mm metallic pompom
- 1⅓" x 1½" wooden book
- Dimensional paints: pearlescent light green and red

Snowman
Gift Basket
Instructions beg
on page 154

Country Santa With Gifts

Place this lovable Santa with stacks of gifts in any small nook or cranny for a touch of old-time country Christmas charm!

Country Santa With Gifts

Design by Deborah Spofford

Materials

- 8" square ¾"-thick wood
- Scroll saw or band saw
- 150-grit sandpaper
- Ceramcoat acrylic paints from Delta Technical Coatings, Inc.:
  Maroon #02-075
  Fleshtone base #02-082
  Pigskin #02-093
  Heritage blue #02-415
  Santa's flesh #02-472
  Olive yellow #02-493
- Series #4300 paintbrushes from Loew-Cornell: #6 and #10 shaders, #5/0 spotter and #3 round
- Split pea
- Liquid wood stain from Delta Technical Coatings, Inc.
- Lint-free cloth
- Matte-finish varnish from Delta Technical Coatings, Inc.
- Fine-line black permanent marking pen
- 3 small brass-head nails
- 1⅔ yards natural nubby yarn or roving
- Tea bag
- ⅔ yard natural jute twine
- 1" square brown paper
- Hot-glue gun

Project Notes

Paint both sides and all edges of wooden Santa and presents, letting painted sections dry before painting adjacent areas or adding painted decorations on top of base coat.

Refer to photo throughout.

Painting

1. Referring to patterns (page 153–154), cut Santa, single gift and two gifts from wood. Sand edges.

2. *Santa:* Thin small amounts of each paint color with water to a transparent consistency. Using #10 shader, base-coat Santa's hat and coat with maroon. Using #6 shader, base-coat face and hands with Santa's flesh, and hat pompom and hat brim with fleshtone base. Using #3 round brush, paint cuffs with fleshtone base. Paint split pea with maroon for nose. Using #5/0 spotter brush, paint two holly leaves on hat brim with olive yellow, and three holly berries with maroon.

3. *Two Gifts:* Using #10 shader and thinned paint mixtures, paint larger present maroon and smaller present pigskin. Using the #5/0 spotter brush, paint small fleshtone stars on the maroon package. Using #6 shader, paint heritage blue stripe for ribbon on pigskin package.

4. *Single Gift:* Using #10 shader, paint present heritage blue. Add a pattern of tiny dots painted in threes using #5/0 spotter and pigskin.

5. When all paint is dry, sand Santa and presents so that some of the paint is removed from edges for a distressed look. Wipe off all dust.

6. Pour wood stain onto a damp cloth; wipe over Santa and presents. Let dry. Brush matte varnish onto Santa and presents; let dry.

Finishing

1. With fine-line marking pen, outline stars, dots and ribbon on presents. Draw curly lines around Santa's cuff, hat pompom and hat trim; add sleeve lines, and dots for Santa's eyes.

2. Hammer brass nails down front of coat for buttons.

3. Wrap yarn around four fingers about 11 times to make a bundle about 2½" wide. Carefully slip yarn loops off fingers. Referring to dashed line on pattern, place line of hot glue on Santa's face; press yarn into glue; let dry. Trim bottom of beard with scissors. Glue a 2" piece of yarn across top of beard for mustache. Glue painted split pea above mustache for nose.

4. Dip tea bag into warm water; lay wet tea bag on beard in several spots to darken yarn for an antique appearance.

5. Tie two small bows of jute twine and glue one atop the maroon and one atop the pigskin gifts. Cut a 9" piece of jute; wrap around heritage blue gift and tie in a bow at the top.

6. Cut gift tag from brown paper; write "Merry Christmas" and draw stitch lines around edges using fine-tip marker. Glue tag to bow on maroon present.

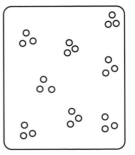

Single Gift

← Apply glue
along this line

Santa

Gift Tag

Two Gifts

W hether filled with pinecones and potpourri or over-flowing with freshly baked goodies, this lovely basket makes an appreciated gift or decoration!

Snowman Gift Basket

Design by Deborah Spofford • Shown on page 152

Materials

- Small pieces of ¼"-thick birch stock
- Scroll saw or band saw
- Sandpaper
- Ceramcoat acrylic paints from Delta Technical Coatings, Inc.:
  Antique white #02-001
  Forest green #02-010
  Pumpkin #02-042
  Coral #02-044
- Paintbrushes: #6 flat and #10/0 detail
- Black fine-line permanent marking pen
- Walnut #53-208 Home Decor gel wood stain from Delta Technical Coatings, Inc.
- Decorative Snow artificial snow paste from Delta Technical Coatings, Inc.
- Small amount of fabric in a country check or print
- Hot-glue gun with wood-glue sticks
- Basket with straight sides (sample is approximately 8½" x 10½")
- Small amount of natural cotton batting

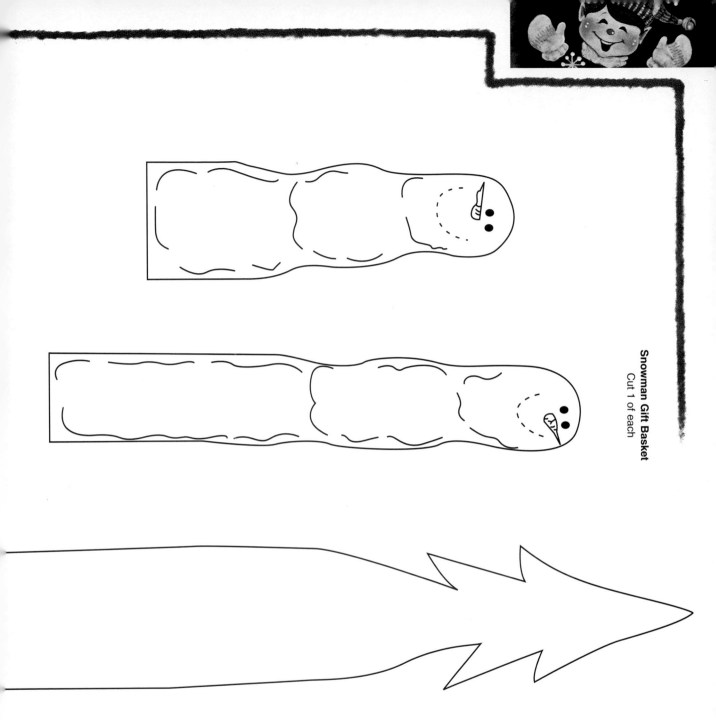

Snowman Gift Basket
Cut 1 of each

Project Note

Refer to photo (page 152) throughout for placement.

Instructions

1. Referring to patterns, cut two snowmen and tree from birch stock; sand edges.

2. Base-coat snowmen with antique white; base-coat tree with forest green. Let paints dry, then sand edges lightly to give each piece a worn look.

3. Using black marking pen, draw eyes, noses and mouths on snowmen. Using #10/0 detail brush, paint snowmen's carrot noses with pumpkin; add cheeks with coral. Let paints dry, then touch up penned-on details as needed, and dot antique white highlights onto eyes and cheeks. Let paints dry thoroughly.

4. Dilute walnut gel stain very thin by adding water. Apply a coat of this wash to snowmen to give them an antiqued appearance; let dry. Dab snow paste onto snowmen and tree as desired; let dry completely.

5. Tear two narrow strips of fabric; tie one around each snowman's neck for scarf.

6. Glue tree and snowmen to side of basket as shown. Glue a "snowdrift" of natural cotton batting to basket at base of snowmen and tree.

7. Tie fabric bow around basket handle. ✎

Celebrate It Christmas • **155**

Project Notes

Red velvet cording is widely available at fabric stores. Dashed lines on pattern pieces indicated stitching lines. Refer to photo throughout for placement.

Armature & Face

1. Cut velvet cording in half; remove white stuffing from inside and insert wire in each piece.

2. Referring to Armature Diagram (page 159), form body, beginning with legs; leave feet unbent at this time. About 5½" up from bottom of wires, twist wires together for about 1½"; these two wires become the arms and neck. Bend one wire up to make a 1" neck loop, then bend out arms; trim arms to 3" in length for now.

3. Referring to pattern (page 159), cut pantyhose square into 3" circle; sew running stitch around outside using carpet thread. Pull thread to gather; stuff pocket with fiberfill. Pull gathering stitch tight and knot off. In center of stuffed circle, make nose by sewing a small circle

*F*rom making gifts to hanging decorations, Santa's little helpers are ever so busy! Craft them tonight to decorate your home for Christmas!

Santa's Elves

Designs by Barbara A. Woolley

Materials
Each Elf

- 1⅛ yards ⅜" red velvet cording (see Project Notes)
- 2 (18") cotton-covered 16-gauge floral wires
- 4" square cut from old pantyhose
- Skin-tone carpet or button thread
- Hand-sewing needle
- Polyester fiberfill about the size of a small apple
- Acrylic paints: red, black and white
- #2 liner paintbrush
- Powdered cosmetic blusher
- Pinking shears
- 9" x 12" green felt
- 9" x 12" Christmas-print fabric
- Sewing threads: red and green
- 3 (½") white flat buttons
- Thick craft glue
- 1 yard 3mm-wide red satin ribbon
- 2 small drapery weights
- 1" bow of plaid fabric ribbon
- Curly Hair winter white #06-200 doll hair from One & Only Creations
- ½" pompom: red, white or green
- Something for elf to hold: miniature Christmas wreath, string of tiny Christmas tree lights, tiny packages, miniature birdhouse, etc.

with tiny running stitches; pull thread tight, being sure to catch some of the stuffing. Knot off and trim thread ends closely.

4. Add facial features, painting mouth with red and eyes with black. When paint is dry, add white highlights to eyes. Dab cheeks with cosmetic blusher.

Clothing

1. Using pinking shears and referring to patterns, cut one jacket from green felt and two shorts from green felt or print fabric; using regular scissors, cut four shoes and four mittens, reversing two, from green felt. Cut two hats from print fabric.

2. *Shorts:* Sew shorts together along side seams and inseam, right sides of felt or fabric facing; turn shorts right side out. Turn hems of shorts up about ¼" with pinked edges on outside. Place shorts on elf; run gathering stitch around waist; pull to secure shorts and knot off tightly.

3. *Jacket:* With scissors cut armholes where noted; fold collar to outside along dotted line shown on pattern. Using red thread, stitch white button to jacket where indicated. Slip jacket on elf, inserting arms through armholes. Overlap edges about ¼" on front with button on top; glue front opening of jacket closed.

4. *Hat:* Lay halves together, right sides facing; using coordinating thread, seam hat together along sides and top. Turn hat right side out. Turn edge of hat under about ½"; secure with a gathering stitch of co-ordinating or contrasting thread about ¼" from edge.

Finishing

1. Tie red satin ribbon in seven ¾" bows and one 1¼" bow. Trim ribbon ends.

2. Using red thread, sew white button to center of each of two shoes; these are shoe tops. Fold ½" feet at ends of legs; sandwich foot between felt shoe top and bottom, inserting one drapery weight in each shoe; glue shoe halves together. Glue small red ribbon bow to shoe at ankle. Repeat for other foot and shoe.

3. Fold ½" hands at ends of arms; sandwich hand between mitten halves and glue mitten in place. Glue small red bow to top of mitten at wrist, and another to bottom of mitten at wrist. Repeat for other hand and mitten.

4. Glue larger red ribbon bow to center front of shorts at waist. Glue remaining small bow to back of jacket, where jacket tails meet. Glue plaid ribbon bow at neckline of jacket, above white button.

5. Following manufacturer's instructions, glue curly hair to elf's head. When glue is dry, position hat on head; pull gathering thread to gather hat as desired; glue in place. Sew pompom to tip of hat.

6. Glue wreath, tree lights, birdhouse or other item to elf's hands as desired.

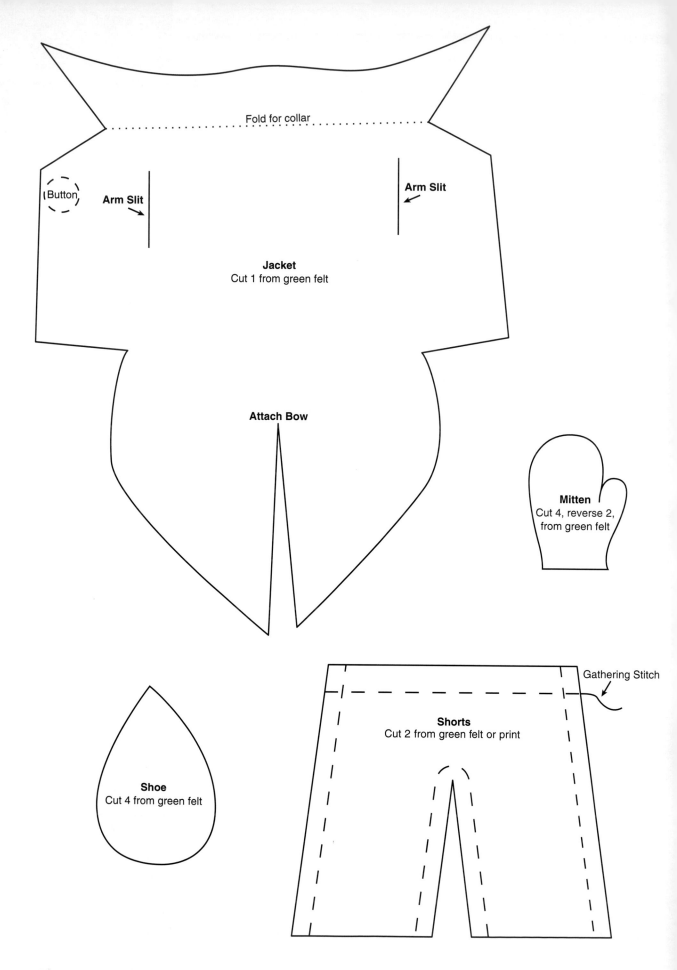

Fold for collar

Button

Arm Slit

Arm Slit

Jacket
Cut 1 from green felt

Attach Bow

Mitten
Cut 4, reverse 2,
from green felt

Shoe
Cut 4 from green felt

Gathering Stitch

Shorts
Cut 2 from green felt or print

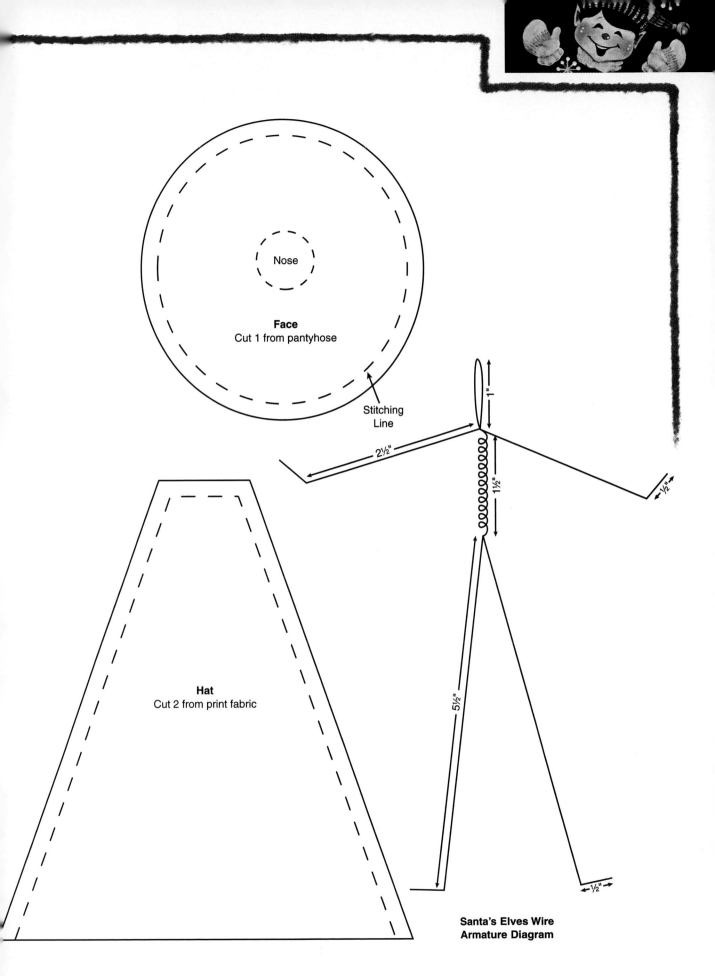

Face
Cut 1 from pantyhose

Nose

Stitching
Line

1"

2½"

1½"

½"

Hat
Cut 2 from print fabric

5½"

½"

**Santa's Elves Wire
Armature Diagram**

Short Santa

1. From double-sided adhesive cut one 3" square, one ¼" x 3" strip, two ½" x 3" strips and one ½" x 5½" strip.

2. Remove paper from one side of 3" adhesive square and press to back of flannel; cut out fabric around adhesive. Remove paper backing; press flannel onto dowel, overlapping ends in back.

3. In same manner, apply remaining adhesive strips to back of plush felt and cut out. Press ¼"-wide strip down center front of dowel; press two ½" x 3" strips around top and bottom of dowel, overlapping ends in back.

4. Referring to hat pattern (page 161), cut two hats from flannel. Leaving ¼" seam allowance, sew pieces together, right sides facing, leaving bottom open. Trim seam allowance to ⅛" and turn hat right side out. Continue as instructed in "Assembly" on page 161.

Medium Santa

1. From double-sided adhesive cut one 3" x 4" rectangle, one ¼" x 4" strip, two ½" x 3" strips and one ½" x 5½" strip.

2. Complete body and hat as instructed in steps 2–4 for Short Santa, substituting 3" x 4" rectangle for 3" square.

Tall Santa

1. From double-sided adhesive cut one 3" x 5" rectangle, one ¼" x 5" strip, two ½" x 3" strips and one ½" x 5½" strip.

2. Complete body and hat

ho can resist these charming stand-up Santas? Dress them with scraps of plaid flannel and fuzzy felt for wintry warmth.

as instructed in steps 2–4 for Small Santa, substituting 3" x 5" rectangle for 3" square.

Assembly

1. Paint two black dots on wooden ball for eyes; let dry. Apply cosmetic blusher to cheeks with cotton swab. Paint half-round bead red (hold bead with a piece of double-stick tape while painting). Paint wooden oval black; let dry.

2. Apply satin-finish varnish to painted wooden ball head and oval base; let dry.

3. Glue painted wooden head to top of dowel; glue bottom of dowel to center of oval base.

4. Cut roving into one 1½" piece and one ½" piece. Spread center of 1½" roving to width of 1¼", leaving ends compact. Glue beard to front of face, pulling and gluing ends to sides of face. Separate ½" piece of roving into three pieces; save two for remaining Santas. Glue one piece to face and beard for mustache.

5. Glue red half-round bead above mustache for nose.

6. Slip hat onto head so back of hat is ¼" from bottom of head bead and front of hat is above eyes. Lightly glue in place. Remove paper from back of remaining ½" x 5½" strip of plush felt. Apply strip to hat and head, covering edge of hat, and overlapping ends in back.

7. Tie each button with two strands of ecru heavy cotton thread; knot on top of button and clip ends to ⅜". Glue one button to tip of

cap; referring to photo, pull tip of hat down slightly and glue to secure. Glue remaining buttons evenly spaced down front felt strip on dowel.

Finishing

Short Santa: Bend greenery into circle and twist ends together. Tie ribbon into small bow; clip ends at an angle and glue to wreath. Glue wreath to side of Santa.

Medium Santa: Fold Osnaburg in half, matching short ends; seam long edges together using ¼" seam allowance and rounding corners slightly. Trim seam allowance to ⅛" and turn bag right side out. Turn raw edge at opening inside ½"; finger-press. Lightly stuff bottom half of sack with fiberfill. Glue in ends of evergreen boughs, twigs and pinecones. Cut berries from pick and glue to boughs. Tie ribbon around bag in a bow ¾" from top of bag; trim ribbon ends at an angle. Glue bag to bottom of Santa and base.

Tall Santa: Paint wooden heart cutout red; let dry. Wrap center of 2" bough around twig ½" from end. Wrap 2½" and 3" boughs around twig in same manner, spacing boughs 1" apart and trimming ends with wire cutters as necessary. Tie ribbon in bow around twig 1½" below bottom bough; trim ribbon ends at an angle. Glue heart near top of tree and glue tree to bottom of Santa and base. ✃

Three Little Santas

Designs by Chris Malone

Materials

Short Santa
- 3" 1³⁄₁₆"-diameter wooden dowel
- 3 (⅜") buttons to complement fabric
- 5" ½"-wide artificial greenery

Medium Santa
- 4" 1³⁄₁₆"-diameter wooden dowel
- 4 (⅜") buttons to complement fabric
- 3½" x 4" piece natural Osnaburg or muslin
- 3 (3") pieces ½"-wide artificial greenery
- 3 (4") ¹⁄₁₆"-diameter twigs
- 4 (½") pinecones
- Red berry floral pick
- Small amount of polyester fiberfill

Tall Santa
- 5" 1³⁄₁₆"-diameter wooden dowel
- 5 (⅜") buttons to complement fabric
- ¾" wooden heart cutout
- ½"-wide artificial greenery: 2", 2½" and 3" pieces
- 6½" ⅜"-diameter twig
- 4 (½") pinecones
- Red berry floral pick
- Small amount of polyester fiberfill

Each Santa
- 5½" x 8¾" sheet PeelnStick double-sided adhesive from Therm O Web
- 5" x 10" checked or plaid flannel fabric
- 2" x 5½" piece antique white plush felt
- Acrylic paints: black and red
- Paintbrush
- 1½" wooden ball knob
- Powdered cosmetic blusher
- Cotton swab
- 6mm half-round wooden bead
- 1¾" x 2" wooden oval
- 2" white wool roving
- Ecru heavy cotton thread
- Satin-finish varnish
- 8" 1¼"-wide red satin ribbon
- Wire cutters
- Double-stick tape
- Low-temperature glue gun

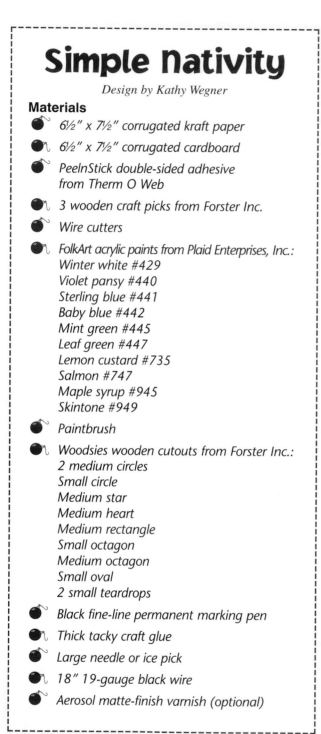

Simple Nativity

Design by Kathy Wegner

Materials

- 6½" x 7½" corrugated kraft paper
- 6½" x 7½" corrugated cardboard
- PeelnStick double-sided adhesive from Therm O Web
- 3 wooden craft picks from Forster Inc.
- Wire cutters
- FolkArt acrylic paints from Plaid Enterprises, Inc.:
  Winter white #429
  Violet pansy #440
  Sterling blue #441
  Baby blue #442
  Mint green #445
  Leaf green #447
  Lemon custard #735
  Salmon #747
  Maple syrup #945
  Skintone #949
- Paintbrush
- Woodsies wooden cutouts from Forster Inc.:
  2 medium circles
  Small circle
  Medium star
  Medium heart
  Medium rectangle
  Small octagon
  Medium octagon
  Small oval
  2 small teardrops
- Black fine-line permanent marking pen
- Thick tacky craft glue
- Large needle or ice pick
- 18" 19-gauge black wire
- Aerosol matte-finish varnish (optional)

*C*elebrate the birth of Jesus with this simple yet decorative Nativity scene.

Instructions

1. Referring to pattern, cut one barn shape from corrugated kraft paper and another from cardboard. Apply double-sided adhesive to cardboard; peel off backing and apply flat side of corrugated kraft paper to cardboard.

2. Referring to craft pick diagrams, clip ends off craft picks as shown, using wire cutters.

3. Paint wooden pieces as follows:

  Winter white—craft picks

  Violet pansy—oval

  Sterling blue—medium octagon

  Baby blue—small octagon

  Mint green—heart

  Leaf green—rectangle

  Lemon custard—star

  Maple syrup—teardrops

  Skintone—medium and small circles

Let paints dry.

4. *Baby Jesus:* Thin salmon paint with water; dab onto small skintone circle for cheeks, referring to face diagrams (page 163). When paint is dry, draw eyes with fine-line marker. Referring to layout diagram (page 163), glue maple syrup teardrops to corrugated surface for manger; glue on pansy oval and Baby Jesus' head.

5. *Mary:* Using additional thinned salmon paint, dab cheeks onto medium skintone circle as shown on face diagrams. Paint on hair using maple syrup paint. When paint is dry, draw eyes with fine-line marker. Referring to layout diagram, glue sterling blue octagon and baby blue octagon to corrugated background; glue painted head on top, overlapping pieces as shown.

6. *Joseph:* Using thinned salmon paint, dab cheeks onto remaining fleshtone circle as shown on face diagrams. Paint on hair and beard using maple syrup paint. When paint is dry, draw eyes with fine-line marker. Referring to layout diagram, glue mint green heart above leaf green rectangle on corrugated background; glue painted head on top, overlapping as shown.

7. *Star:* Glue star and rays (white craft picks) to top of barn as shown.

8. Punch two holes through barn where indicated. Spray Nativity with varnish if desired; let dry.

9. Thread wire through holes for hanger, coiling ends to secure hanger in place. ✒

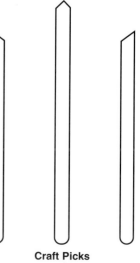

Craft Picks
Trim as shown

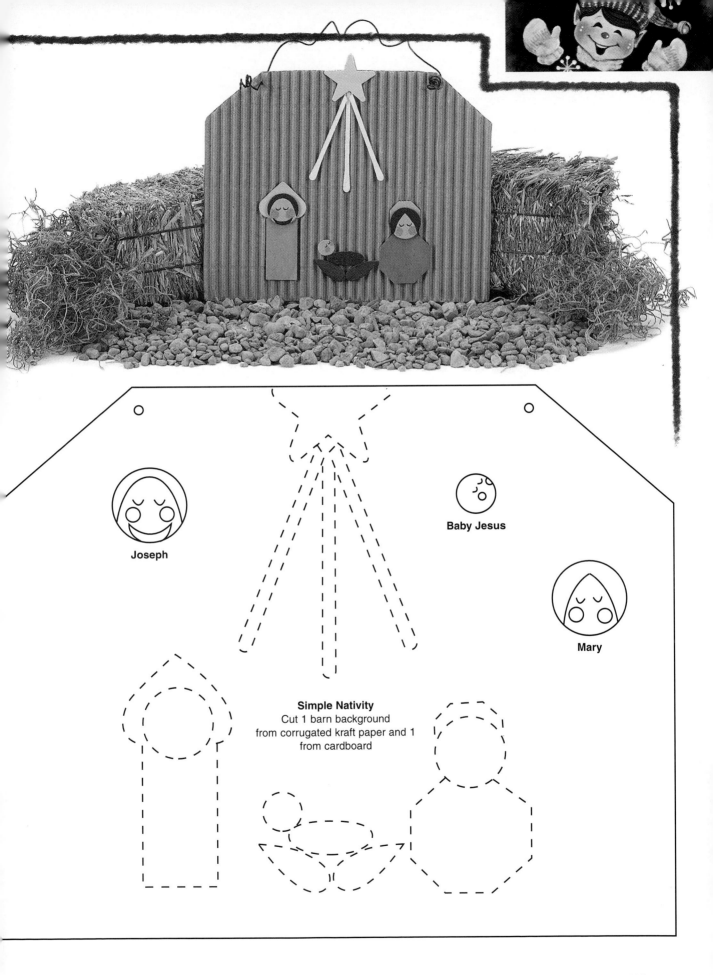

Joseph

Baby Jesus

Mary

Simple Nativity
Cut 1 barn background
from corrugated kraft paper and 1
from cardboard

*I*f winter is your favorite season of the year, then you'll love crafting this colorful tree adorned with snowmen, snowflakes and mittens!

Let It Snow Christmas Tree

Design by Kathy Wegner

Materials

- Rainbow Classic Felt from Kunin Felt:
  7" x 9" apple green
  9" x 12" pirate green
  15" square kelly green
  3" x 2" each of red, orange, yellow, lime, blueberry bash, grape and shocking pink
- Craft foam:
  3½" x 5½" yellow
  Small piece of orange
- 12" x 5" Styrofoam plastic-foam cone from Dow Chemical Company
- Thick tacky glue
- White pompoms: 12 each ½" and 1"
- 12 (3½") lengths yarn in assorted colors to match or coordinate with felt colors
- 24 black seed beads
- 14 (24mm) white snowflake sequins
- Toothpick or skewer

Instructions

1. Referring to patterns (pages 165 and 166), cut one top tree piece from apple green, one middle tree piece from pirate green and one bottom tree piece from kelly green. Cut Star A and B from yellow craft foam; cut two mittens from each of the 3" x 2" felt pieces to make a total of 14 mittens.

2. Trace around bottom of cone onto leftover kelly green felt; cut out and glue felt to bottom of cone.

3. Glue kelly green bottom piece around bottom of cone; trim any excess where edges meet. Glue pirate green middle piece above bottom piece, aligning seam with seam on bottom piece; let curved parts lap over bottom piece, but don't glue them down. Trim excess where sides meet. Glue apple green top piece

over middle piece, letting extra felt stick up over tip of cone. Let glue dry.

4. Push hole straight down into top of cone with pencil. Dab glue into hole; push excess felt into hole with pencil.

5. For each snowman, glue a ½" pompom atop a 1" pompom; let dry. Tie a knot in each end of a 3½" yarn piece; glue around snowman's neck. Cut a sliver of orange craft foam and glue on for carrot-shaped nose. Glue two seed beads for eyes. Repeat with remaining pompoms, yarn, foam and beads.

6. Attach mittens randomly to tree, applying glue only to cuff area. Glue snowmen on tree between mittens; glue on snowflake sequins randomly in empty spaces. Let glue dry.

7. Cut slits in yellow foam stars where indicated; slide star halves together; glue in place and let dry.

8. Dab glue onto top of tree. Using a toothpick or skewer, push star tabs into top of tree.

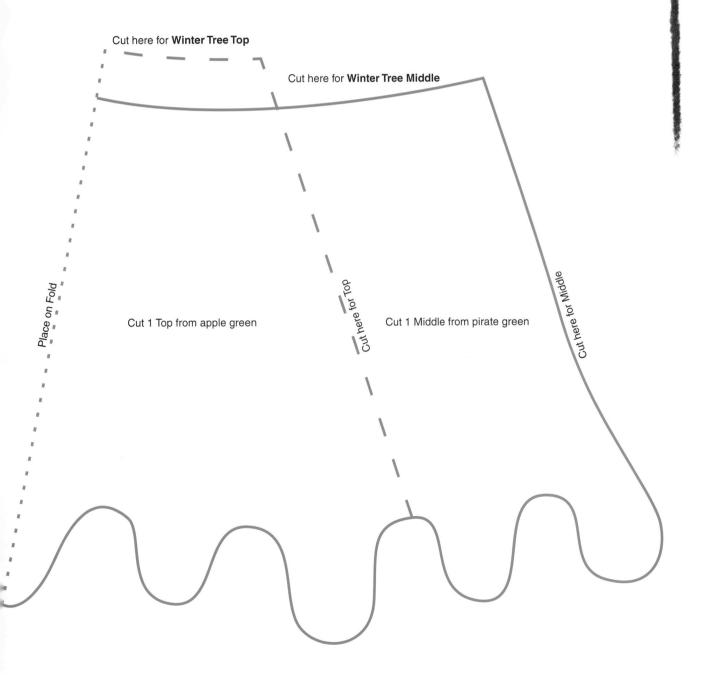

Cut here for **Winter Tree Top**

Cut here for **Winter Tree Middle**

Place on Fold

Cut here for Top

Cut here for Middle

Cut 1 Top from apple green

Cut 1 Middle from pirate green

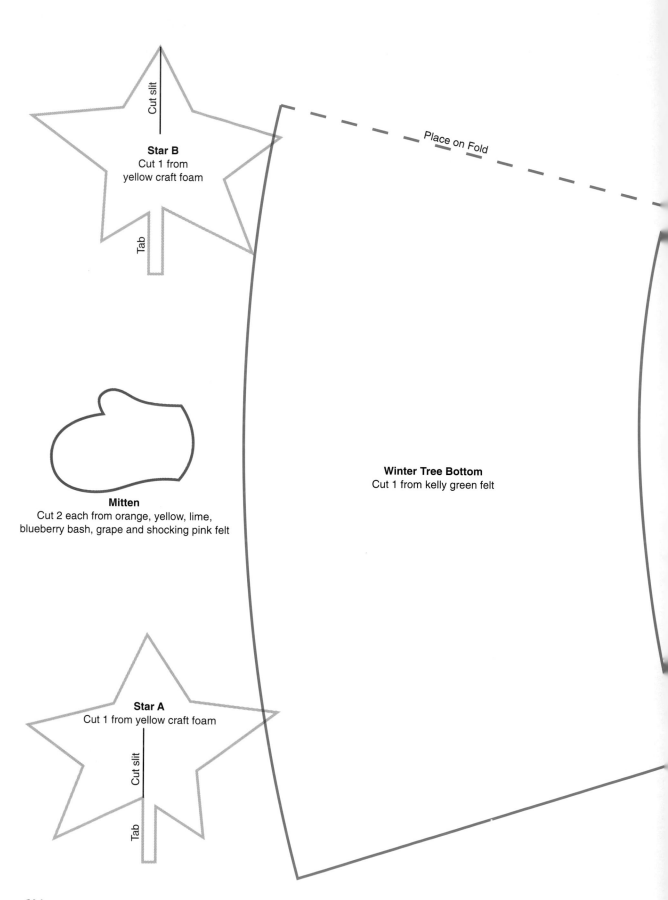

Star B
Cut 1 from
yellow craft foam

Cut slit

Tab

Place on Fold

Mitten
Cut 2 each from orange, yellow, lime,
blueberry bash, grape and shocking pink felt

Winter Tree Bottom
Cut 1 from kelly green felt

Star A
Cut 1 from yellow craft foam

Cut slit

Tab

Snowman Light

Design by Barbara A. Woolley

Materials

- 6" round wooden base
- Fine- to medium-grit sandpaper
- Acrylic craft paints: orange and dark green
- Paintbrush
- Water-base varnish
- 5¾" circle red or green felt
- White tacky glue
- 1" twig or stick whittled into a carrot shape
- ¼ yard Warm & Natural batting from Warm Products, Inc.
- Sewing machine or hand-sewing needle
- Sewing threads: white, red and green
- Electric welcome light
- Polyester fiberfill
- 2" Styrofoam plastic-foam ball from Dow Chemical Company
- Hot-glue gun
- 6" x 3" piece knit fabric
- 6" piece narrow ribbon or gold cord
- 2 (¾") pompoms in color to coordinate with fabric
- 2 (8mm) black beads
- Powdered cosmetic blusher
- Black fine-line permanent marking pen
- Buttons: 7 red, 7 white, 4 green and 1 heart-shape
- 6-strand embroidery floss: red and green
- 2 (5") twigs for arms
- 3" grapevine or pine wreath
- 1½" birdhouse on a stick
- Assorted embellishments: miniature birds, tiny packages and candy canes, miniature holly leaves, tiny ribbon bows, etc.
- Decorative Snow artificial snow paste by Delta Technical Coatings, Inc.
- Holiday print, plaid or checked fabric: ¼ yard 12" x 2" strip
- Design-A-Shade 2" x 5" x 4" self-adhesive lamp shade from Northland Designs
- ¾ yard trim for shade

Place this adorable snowman night-light in a window to light up your heart and home during the winter season.

Project Notes

Refer to photo throughout for placement.

Use hot glue gun to attach snowman to base and arms to snowman. Use tacky glue for remainder of project construction.

Instructions

1. Sand wooden base; paint with green paint and let dry. Coat with water-base varnish; let dry. Glue felt circle to bottom of wooden base.

2. Paint whittled twig orange; let dry.

3. Referring to pattern (page 168), cut two snowman shapes from batting. Using machine or sewing by hand, stitch pieces together along sides, right sides facing, leaving 2" openings at top and bottom for turning. Turn snowman right side out. By hand, sew running gathering stitches around both openings, leaving long thread ends for tying off later.

4. Stuff body loosely; insert candlestick from bottom through top; candle should extend about 6" above top of snowman's head. Flatten one side of plastic-foam ball by pressing it against a hard surface; position opposite side against candle base inside snowman; candle will rest atop ball and flat side of ball will rest on base. Stabilize candlestick and ball by stuffing snowman very firmly around them.

5. Pull running stitches until openings are tightly gathered (electrical cord will protrude from bottom opening); knot off securely and clip thread ends.

6. Glue edges of snowman's top opening to candlestick; hot-glue bottom of stuffed snowman securely to wooden base.

7. To make hat, sew knit fabric into a tube by seaming 3" sides together; turn right side out. Sew a gathering stitch around one edge; this will be top of hat. Fold bottom edge up to make a cuff; fit hat over candlestick onto snowman's head. Pull gathering stitch tightly around candlestick; knot off and clip thread ends. Glue hat to snowman's head and lamp.

8. Hold cording or ribbon over top of head for earmuffs wire; glue ends to sides of head. Glue a pompom over each end for earmuffs.

9. Glue beads in place for eyes; apply blusher to cheeks, and add x's with marking pen for mouth. Glue base of painted orange twig to face for nose.

10. Tie simple overhand knots through green buttons using red embroidery floss; clip thread ends to about ¼". Glue buttons down front of snowman; glue on heart-shaped button.

11. Hot-glue twigs in place for arms. Decorate wreath and birdhouse as desired

with embellishments, and add to snowman.

12. Following manufacturer's instructions, apply snow paste to snowman's arms and hat, to wreath, and around base. Set other

embellishments—small package, candy canes, etc.—into still-wet snow at base of snowman, and add touches of snow. Let dry.

13. Tie fabric strip around snowman's neck for scarf.

14. Following shade manufacturer's instructions, cover shade with ¼ yard fabric. Glue trim around top and bottom edges of lamp shade, matching seams of shade to seam in

fabric. Tie floss through remaining buttons as in step 10 using red floss in white buttons and green floss in red buttons; glue buttons randomly onto lamp shade. ✒

O Holy Night Nativity

Design by Barbara A. Woolley

Materials

- 5 (2") unpainted wooden doll pins
- Acrylic paints: dark and light skin tones, metallic gold, red and white
- Small paintbrush
- Black fine-line permanent marking pen
- Toothpick or pin
- 5 skin-tone pipe cleaners
- White tacky glue
- Hot-glue gun
- Small bits of yarn or doll hair
- Scraps of fabrics and trims
- 3 (½") unpainted wooden spools
- Small beads and buttons
- 8mm natural wooden bead
- Small piece of polyester fiberfill
- Craft foam:
  7" x 2½" piece brown
  1½" square yellow
- Cinnamon sticks: at least 15 (7") sticks and several 2"–3" sticks
- Sheet moss
- Pinking shears

Join the Three Wise Men as they come to give praise to the new-born Messiah with this heart-warming Nativity scene.

Project Notes

Refer to photo throughout for placement.

Save fabrics from men's ties for crafting projects. Tie fabric was used for this project.

Mary, Joseph and the Wise Men are made in basically the same manner; add variety by choosing different fabrics and embellishments. See General Instructions below to make each of these adult characters. Separate instructions for Baby Jesus follow.

General Instructions

1. Paint the round ball portion on top of clothespin with paint in desired skin tone; let dry. Using permanent marker, draw on facial features. If desired, paint on rosy cheeks using red paint thinned with water. Add white paint highlights to eyes, applying tiny drops of white with a pin or toothpick.

2. For each figure, use a 6" section cut from a pipe cleaner; wrap around neck of doll pin for arms.

3. Glue on tiny bits of hair in desired colors. Add beards to some of the male characters as desired.

4. Referring to patterns (page 170) and using pinking shears, cut a robe from each fabric used for Mary, Joseph and Wise Men. With wrong sides of fabric facing, sew side and underarm seams; turn robe right side out.

5. Dress doll, hot-gluing robe in place. If you want it to look like the doll is wearing something under the robe, cut the robe up the center and glue a scrap of fabric in the opening. Refer to Joseph in photo.

6. Add ribbon, bows, buttons and other embellishments as desired.

7. Make a head scarf for Mary by cutting fabric to fit with pinking shears and hot-gluing in place.

8. Make crowns for Wise Men by gluing a circlet of

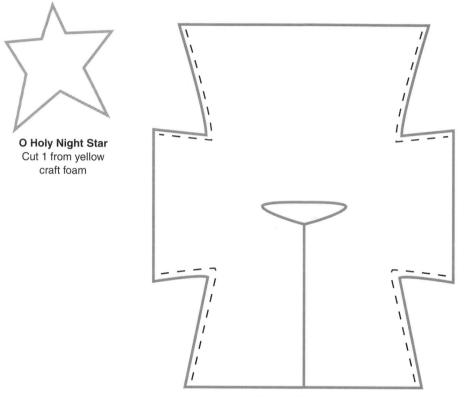

O Holy Night Star
Cut 1 from yellow
craft foam

O Holy Night Robe
Cut 1 for each adult
figure

gold braid trim or gold paper around head.

9. To make the Wise Men's gifts, paint miniature spools gold and embellish as desired—with gold or silver beads, gold or silver cord or trims, faux jewels, beads, etc. Hot-glue gifts to Wise Men's hands.

Baby Jesus

1. Paint 8mm wooden bead with desired paint; let dry.

Draw on facial features with marking pen, and add cheeks with diluted red paint. Glue a few wisps of hair to head, and add a halo of a tiny circlet of gold cord.

2. For body, wrap a nickel-size bit of stuffing in a scrap of fabric; hot-glue head to top.

Stable & Manger

1. Use brown craft foam as base; hot-glue 7" cinnamon sticks to it to cover. Build a

"back wall" of 7" cinnamon sticks perpendicular to base; glue two shorter sticks upright to wall for braces. Glue base of wall and braces to back of base.

2. Fill in gaps between sticks with pieces of sheet moss. Cut star from yellow craft foam; add border with marking pen, and glue star to top center of stable's back wall.

3. For manger, trim several narrower shorter cinnamon sticks to about 1½". Make two X's by crossing two short cinnamon sticks; hot-glue in place. These will be ends of manger. Complete manger by gluing additional shorter sticks in top V of end pieces. Add bits of sheet moss.

4. Glue manger, Mary, Joseph, Baby Jesus and Wise Men in place as desired.

Whether you use these easy-to-craft bags as decorations in a corner or near your tree, or actually fill them with gifts, they're sure to add holiday charm to your home!

Santa's Bags

Design by Debbie Williams • Shown on page 172

Materials
- Stiff cardboard
- Red bags with ties from BagWorks, Inc.:
  8" x 12" #2308
  12" x 15½" #2312
  16" x 17" #2316
- String of stars #95-113-0012 Stencil Magic pre-cut stencil from Delta Technical Coatings, Inc.
- Masking tape
- Metallic gold #90-201-0059 Stencil Magic stencil paint creme from Delta Technical Coatings, Inc.
- Stencil Magic stencil brushes from Delta Technical Coatings, Inc.:
  ¼" #98-300-0008
  ⅝" #98-302-0008
- Freezer paper or disposable palette paper
- Sewing needle
- Red sewing thread
- 6 (13mm) gold jingle bells
- Approximately 10 ounces polyester fiberfill

Project Notes
Prewashing fabric bags is not necessary; smooth out any wrinkles with a warm iron before beginning.

It is not necessary to heat-set paint on stenciled bags, but do wait at least 10 days before laundering bags. To launder, remove stuffing, turn bags inside out and wash bags separately in cold water using mild soap. Line-dry. If ironing is necessary, turn inside out to iron.

Stenciling
1. Cut a piece of cardboard to fit inside each bag so that bag surface will lie smoothly and paint will not bleed through from front to back.

2. Cover "string" areas on both sides of stencil with pieces of masking tape, leaving only stars open.

3. Remove film from stencil creme by placing corner of folded paper towel firmly on paint surface and twisting as if unscrewing a lid. The dry film of paint will peel off; discard film.

4. To stencil, use very little paint on a dry stencil brush appropriately sized for opening being stenciled. Touch brush to paint creme and press lightly; blot off any excess paint on a paper towel by pressing brush in a circular motion. Begin by positioning stencil horizontally across each bag. Firmly holding the stencil in place, use the stencil brushes to apply the paint creme to each star in a circular motion.

5. Randomly fill in remaining areas with stars, repositioning stencil as needed.

6. Mask a stripe for painted border by applying masking tape along top hem seam line. Press firmly along tape to prevent any leakage.

7. Pull cardboard partway out of bag so that 1"–2" extends beyond bag opening. Place a piece of disposable palette or freezer paper inside bag opening leaving 1"–2" extending beyond opening.

8. Using ⅝" stencil brush, paint border using same circular motion as for stencils. When one side of bag is completed, reverse and paint other side, taking care not to smear previously painted area. If you accidentally apply paint to the wrong area, press sticky side of a piece of masking tape over the unwanted paint one or more times until paint is removed.

Finishing
1. Tie knot ⅜" from end of each string on each bag. Using red thread and needle, sew jingle bell at end of each tie about ⅛" from edge. Trim loose threads.

2. Fill each bag to tie strings with fiberfill. Gather top edge of each bag in pleated fashion. Bring ends of tie string forward and tie in simple bow on small and medium bags. Tie knot on largest bag. Tie all strings so that jingle bells face and hang forward.

Source List

3M
Building 304-01-01
3M Center
St. Paul, MN 55144-1000
(800) 364-3577

Adhesive Technologies Inc.
3 Merrill Industrial Dr.
Hampton, NH 03842-1995
(800) 458-3486
www.adhesivetech.com

Aleene's, a division of
Duncan Enterprises
5673 E. Shields Ave.
Fresno, CA 93727
(800) 438-6226

B&B Products Inc.
P.O. Box 428
Allendale, SC 29810
(888) 382-4255
Fax: (877) 329-3824

Beacon Chemical/
Signature Mktg. & Mfg.
P.O. Box 427
Wyckoff, NJ 07481
(800) 865-7238

The Beadery
P.O. Box 178
Hope Valley, RI 02832
(401) 539-2432

Blumenthal Lansing Co.
1929 Main St.
Lansing, IA 52151
(800) 553-4158

Bucilla
1 Oak Ridge Rd.
Humboldt Industrial Park
Hazleton, PA 18201-9764
(800) 233-3239

Charles Craft Inc.
P.O. Box 1049
Laurinburg, NC 28353
(910) 276-4721

Chartpak
1 River Rd.
Leeds, MA 01053
(800) 628-1910

Coats & Clark
Consumer Service
P.O. Box 12229
Greenville, SC 29612-0229
(800) 648-1479
www.coatsandclark.com

Creative Beginnings
P.O. Box 1330
Morro Bay, CA 93442
(800) 367-1739

Creative Chi
8608 Kratz Lane
Baltimore, MD 21244
(410) 922-9110

Darice Inc.
Mail-order source:
Bolek's
P.O. Box 465
330 N. Tuscarawas Ave.
Dover, OH 44622
(330) 364-8878

DecoArt
P.O. Box 386
Stanford, KY 40484
(800) 367-3047

Delta Technical Coatings Inc.
2550 Pellissier Pl.
Whittier, CA 90601-1505
(800) 423-4135

DMC Corp.
Hackensack Ave. Bldg. 10A
South Kearny, NJ 07032-4688
(800) 275-4117
www.dmcusa.com

Duncan Enterprises
5673 E. Shields Ave.
Fresno, CA 93727
(559) 291-4444
www.duncan-enterprises.com

Fibre-Craft Materials Corp.
Mail-order source:
Kirchen Bros.
P.O. Box 1016
Skokie, IL 60076
(800) 378-5024

Forster Inc./Diamond Brands
1800 Cloquet Ave.
Cloquet, MN 55720
(218) 879-6700

Gay Bowles Sales Inc.
P.O. Box 1060
Janesville, WI 53545
(800) 447-1332

Golden Natural /
Silver Brush Ltd.
P.O. Box 414
Windsor Industrial Park #18-E
92 N. Main St.
Windsor, NJ 08561-0414
(609) 443-4900

Hair HookUps
200 S. Marion Rd.
Sioux Falls, SD 57107
(605) 357-9306
www.hairhookup.com

International Papers/Strathmore
Artist Products
39 S. Broad St.
Westfield, MA 01085
(800) 353-0375

Jesse James & Co.
615 N. New St.
Allentown, PA 18102
(610) 435-7899

Kreinik Mfg. Co. Inc.
3601 Timanus Ln., Suite 101
Baltimore, MD 21244
(800) 537-2166

Kunin Felt Co./Foss Mfg. Co. Inc.
P.O. Box 5000
Hampton, NH 03842-5000
(800) 292-7900

Loew-Cornell Inc.
563 Chestnut Ave.
Teaneck, NJ 07666
(201) 836-7070

Madeira Threads
9613 N.E. Colefax St.
Portland, OR 97220-1232
(800) 542-4727

Midwest Products Co. Inc.
P.O. Box 564
Hobart, IN 46342
(219) 942-1134

MPR Associates Inc.
P.O. Box 7343
High Point, NC 27264
(800) 454-3331

Northland Designs/Wisconsin
Lighting
800 Wisconsin St., Suite D02-104
Eau Claire, WI 54703-3598
(715) 834-8707
Fax: (715) 834-2608

One & Only Creations
P.O. Box 2730
Napa, CA 94558
(800) 262-6768

Paper Pizazz
Hot Off The Press Inc.
1250 N.W. Third
Canby, OR 97013
(503) 266-9102

Pellon Division
Freudenberg Nonwovens
1040 Avenue of the Americas, 14th
Floor
New York, NY 10018
(800) 248-5938

Plaid Enterprises Inc.
1649 International Ct.
Norcross, GA 30093
(800) 842-4197
www.plaidonline.com

Shrinky Dinks/K & B Innovations
II Inc.
P.O. Box 223
North Lake, WI 53064
(414) 966-0305
Fax: (414) 966-0306
www.shrinkydinks.com

Speedball Art Products
P.O. Box 5157
Statesville, NC 28687
(800) 898-7224

Therm O Web
770 Glenn Ave.
Wheeling, IL 60090
(847) 520-5200

Tulip, a division of
Duncan Enterprises
5673 E. Shields Ave.
Fresno, CA 93727
(800) 438-6226

Uchida of America, Corp.
3535 Del Amo Blvd.
Torrance, CA 90503
(800) 541-5877

Walnut Hollow Farm Inc.
1409 State Rd. 23
Dodgeville, WI 53533-2112
(800) 950-5101

The Warm Company
954 E. Union St.
Seattle, WA 98122
(800) 234-WARM

West Coast Wood Craft Supplies
1256 Alderney Ct.
Oceanside, CA 92054
(800) 515-9663

Westrim Crafts/Western
Trimming Corp.
9667 Canoga Ave.
Chatsworth, CA 91311
(818) 998-8550

Westwater Industries Inc.
187 Mill Lane
Mountainside, NJ 07092
(908) 654-8871

Wimpole Street Creations
Mail-order source:
Barrett House
P.O. Box 540585
North Salt Lake, UT 84054-0585
(801) 299-0700

Wizards of Wood
918 S. Walnut
Bucyrus, OH 44820

Woodworks
4521 Anderson Blvd.
Forth Worth, TX 76117
(817) 581-5230

Wrights
P.O. Box 398
West Warren, MA 01092
(413) 436-7732 Ext. 445

Zigcraft Woodwork Inc.
220 Myrtle Ave.
Boonton, NJ 07005
(973) 331-9074

Zweigart/Joan Toggitt Ltd.
2 Riverview Dr.
Somerset, NJ 08873
(732) 271-1949
Fax: (732) 271-0758

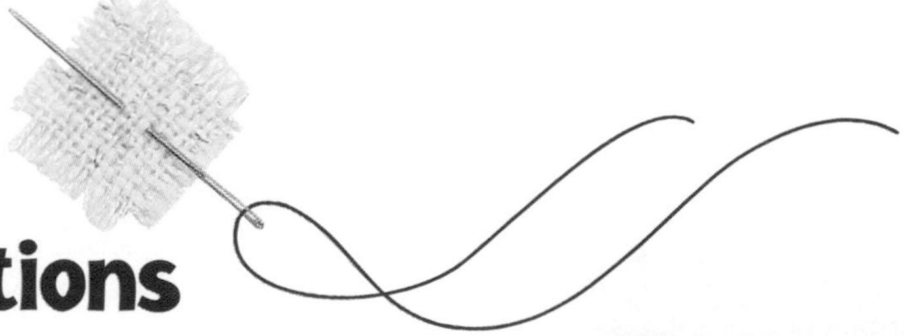

General Instructions

Materials List

In addition to the materials listed for each craft, some of the following crafting supplies may be needed to complete your projects. No doubt most of these are already on hand in your "treasure chest" of crafting aids. If not, you may want to gather them now so that you'll be able to complete each design quickly and without a hitch!

General Crafts

- Scissors
- Pencil
- Ruler
- Tracing paper
- Craft knife
- Heavy-duty craft cutters or wire nippers

Painted Items

- Paper towels
- Paper or plastic foam plate or tray to use as a disposable pain palette for holding and mixing paints
- Plastic—a garbage bag, grocery sack etc.—to protect you work surface
- Container of water for rinsing and cleanin brushes

Fabric Projects

- Iron and ironing board
- Pressing cloth
- Basic sewing notions
- Rotary cutter and self-healing mat
- Air-soluble markers
- Tailor's chalk

Needlework Designs

- Embroidery scissors
- Iron and ironing board
- Thick terry towel
- Air-soluble markers
- Tailor's chalk

Reproducing Patterns & Templates

The patterns provided in this book are shown right side up, as they should look on the finished project; a few oversize patterns that need to be enlarged are clearly marked. Photocopiers with enlarging capabilities are readily available at copy stores and office supply stores. Simply copy the page, setting the photocopier to enlarge the pattern to the percentage indicated.

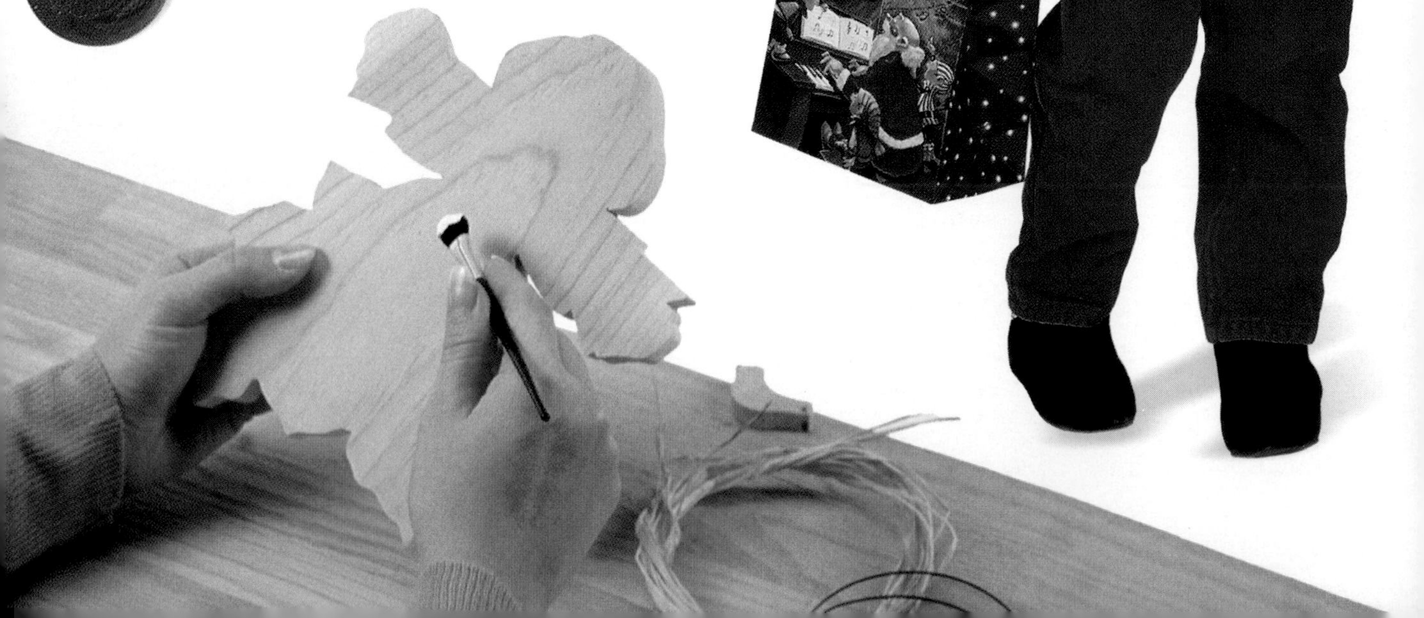

Patterns that do not need to be enlarged may be reproduced simply by placing a piece of tracing paper or vellum over the pattern in the book, and tracing the outlines carefully with a pencil or other marker.

Once you've copied your pattern pieces, cut them out and use these pieces as templates to trace around. Secure them as needed with pins or pattern weights.

If you plan to reuse the patterns or if the patterns are more intricate, with sharp points, etc., make sturdier templates by gluing the copied page of patterns onto heavy cardboard or template plastic. Let the glue dry, then cut out the pieces using a craft knife.

Depending on the application, it may be preferable to trace the patterns onto the *wrong* side of the fabric or other material so that no tracing lines will be visible from the front; in this case, make sure you place the *right* side of the pattern piece against the *wrong* side of the fabric, paper or other material so that the piece will face the right direction when it is cut out.

Using Transfer Paper

Some projects recommend transferring patterns to wood or another material with transfer paper. Read the manufacturer's instructions before beginning.

Lay tracing paper over the printed pattern and trace it carefully. Then place transfer paper, transfer side down, on wood or other material to be marked. Lay traced pattern on top. Secure layers with low-tack masking tape or tacks to keep pattern and transfer paper from shifting while you work.

Using a stylus, pen or other marking implement, retrace the pattern lines using smooth, even pressure to transfer design onto surface.

Working With Fabrics

Read instructions carefully; take seam allowances into consideration when cutting fabrics.

If colorfastness is a concern, launder fabrics first without using fabric softener. Press with an iron before using. Keep an iron and ironing board at hand to press seams and pattern pieces as you work.

Pattern markings may be transferred to fabrics with air-soluble markers or tailor's chalk. For permanent markings on fabric, use the specific pens and paints listed with each project. It is a good idea to always test the pen or marker on a scrap of fabric to check for bleeding, etc.

Painted Designs

Disposable paper or plastic foam plates, including supermarket meat trays, make good palettes for pouring and mixing paints.

The success of a painted project often depends a great deal on the care taken in the initial preparations, including sanding, applying primer, and/or applying a base coat of color. Follow instructions carefully in this regard.

Take special care when painting sections adjacent to different colors; allow the first color to dry so that the second will not run or mix. When adding designs atop a painted base, let the base coat dry thoroughly first.

If you will be mixing media, such as drawing with marking pens on a painted surface, test the process and your materials on scraps to make sure there will be no unsightly running or bleeding.

Keep your work surface and your tools clean. Clean brushes promptly in the manner recommended by the paint manufacturer; many acrylics can be cleaned up with soap and water, while other paints may require a solvent of some kind. Suspend your paintbrushes by their handles to dry so that the cleaning fluid drains out completely without bending the bristles. ✒

Special Thanks

I'd like to thank the following designers whose original designs are featured in this publication. We at House of White Birches are both pleased and honored to include their work in this volume of delightful Christmas crafts. —editor

Victoria Adams Brown
Glittery Vest

Betty Auth
Country Wooden Ornaments

Mary Ayres
Santa Centerpiece

Paula Bales
Holly Centerpiece, Quick-as-a-Wink Ornaments, Santa Gift Bag, Spectacled Santa

Sharon Barrett
One Glorious Night Pillow

Joan Beiriger
Geometric Cross-Stitch Ornaments

Jacqueline Bessner
Jingles the Reindeer

Vicki Blizzard
Santa Pocket Ornaments

Janna Britton
Gingerbread & Snowflake Wreath

Deborah Brooks
Little Lady Bracelets

Mary T. Cosgrove
Christmas Wreath Tote Bag, Pet Treat Toppers

Creative Chi
Christmas Candle Holder, Cinnamon Candle Tree, Cracker Favors, Elegant Christmas Bow, Nature's Bounty Christmas Tree, Nature's Beauty Ornaments, Nature's Gift Boxes, Pinecone Accents Jewelry Boxes, Potpourri Basket, Pressed-Flower Holiday Cards

E. Wayne Fox
Country Christmas Tree Magnet

Bev George
Fridgie Friends

Sandra Graham Smith
Guardian Angels

Crystal Harris Ogle
Pop-Up Holiday Bags, Quick-as-a-Wink Place Cards

Leslie Hartsock
Fabric-Covered Ornaments

Nancy Hearne
Ho Ho Ho Bib

Vivian Holland-Medina
Holly & Berries Wreath, Pearls & Holly Gift Set

Judi Kauffman
Christmas Carol Barrette, Elegant Christmas Combo

Sandy Laipply
Watch It Snow

Blanche Lind
Botanical Cards

Chris Malone
Cheery Snowman Ornaments, Folk-Art Ornaments, Furry Friends Stockings, Rainbow Angels, Santa Star Gift Box, Three Little Santas

Sandra McCooey
Poinsettia Cross

Betty Morris
Shrinky Dink Napkin Rings

Helen Rafson
Christmas Tic-Tac-Toe, Gingerbread Kids

Maggie Rampy
Holiday Carafe

Delores Ruzicka
Cardinal Creations, Necktie Angels, Winter Friends Gift Pots,

Phyllis Sandford
Friendly Snowman Box

Debi Schmitz
Christmas Kitten Puppet Purse, Reindeer Plant Poke

Susan Schultz
Dainty Florals Switchplate Cover, Touch of Gold Table Set, Victorian Potpourri Box

Deborah Spofford
Country Santa With Gifts, Paper-Craft Gift Bag & Tag, Paper-Craft Ornaments, Plaid Paper Ornaments, Snowman Gift Basket

Bonnie Stephens
Ornament Boxes

Charlyne Stewart
Christmas Confections Jacket, Cowboy Boot Stockings

Kathy Wegner
Columbia Star Card, Happy Holidays Postcards, Simple Nativity, String of Ornaments

Beth Wheeler
Vintage Treasure Box

Angie Wilhite
Pine Tree Gift Bag, The Littlest Christmas Vest

Debbie Williams
Santa's Bags, Snow Characters Sweatshirts, Stardust Stocking

Barbara A. Woolley
Brown-Bag Pins, Country Snowman Table Set, Friendship Ornaments, Holiday Mouse Pads, Jingle Bell Jewelry, Li'l Choir Girls, O Tannenbaum Sweatshirt, Santa's Elves, Snowman Light, O Holy Night Nativity, Snowman Pin